UNDERSTANDING THE
PROCESS OF PURPOSE

RICHARD PINDER

Pneuma Life

UNDERSTANDING THE
PROCESS OF PURPOSE

Pneuma Life Publishing
4423 Forbes Blvd.
Lanham, MD 20706-1843
301-577-4052
Internet: http://www.pneumalife.com

Copyright © 2002 by
Printed in the United States of America
ISBN: 1-56229-191-2

Table of Contents

Foreword

Introduction

Foreword

The greatest discovery in life is the discovery of personal purpose and destiny. The most important thing in life is the pursuit and fulfillment of that purpose. Therefore, knowledge and understanding of the processes to that fulfillment is the most critical and must be the concern of every individual.

There is no greatest discovery of personal purpose. The greatest tragedy in life is not death, but life without a purpose. The discovery of purpose is the heart of life and the revelation that gives life meaning and value. Without purpose life has no relevance and time has no reason. What is purpose? Purpose is defined as the original reason for the creation of a thing. It is the original intent for the existence of a thing. In essence, purpose is why a product was created. Purpose is the end for which the means exists. Thus purpose is the only true source of meaning and fulfillment in life.

For many years now I have taught, counseled and researched this subject of purpose and meaning to millions of people and am convinced that until an individual discovers a sense of purpose and destiny in their lives, living is nothing but an aimless experiment in daily frustration. I also contend that most of the anti-social behavior, violent crimes and destructive substances abuse are a direct result of the absence of a sense of purpose in the lives of members of our societies. The discovery of a sense of purpose and destiny produces a spirit of responsibility, discipline and order in life.

It is said that the poorest man in the world is the man without a dream. If this is true, then the most frustrated man in the world is the man with a dream that never becomes a reality. Knowing the end of a journey but not knowing the way to get there is an exercise in disillusionment. We all need help in getting to the end of our dream and arrive at our destiny. In essence we need a plan, a life's map.

Dr. Richard Pinder in *Understanding the Process of Purpose*, provides the missing link to knowing your dream and it's fulfillment. The content of this work is an imperative for the individual who wants to achieve his or her ultimate goals in life. Dr. Pinder, with his simple, yet profound approach to this most important subject, provides practical steps and easy to understand principles as an action plan to take you to fulfillment of your purpose. Dr. Pinder leaps over complicated theoretical and philosophical jargon to present user-friendly concepts anyone can apply. His progressive line on line delivery of action oriented directions for the reader is like a manual for life.

Understanding the Process of Purpose, is a natural companion book to my earlier published work, *In Pursuit of Purpose*, and provides the next step in the process of fulfilling your personal and corporate purpose.

I recommend the work highly and believe it will be the key to filling the gap between knowing your purpose and destiny and getting there. Every one who desires to live a full life, maximize their potential and make a lasting impact on their generation will find this book a necessary part of the process. Read each page and peel the wisdom from every paragraph. The wisdom contained in this book will take you leap years forward to your dream and save you many unnecessary mistakes and regrets through the process.

Understanding the Process of Purpose will become a classic in the lives of thousands of purpose-driven lives and a must for every library. Open these pages, read with an open mind, embrace the practical principles and take action today... if you do, I'll see you at the end of your dream.

Dr. Myles Munroe
CEO/President
BFM Group of Companies

Introduction

"There is a time for everything" Eccl. 3:1

One day I was working out in my backyard and a small, unsightly creature caught my eyes. On closer examination I realized it was a caterpillar. It was actually a butterfly in its infancy stage, but at this point it didn't look anything like the beautiful, intricate insect it would eventually become. As I considered this marvel of nature, I realized that in many ways all of us are like the caterpillar. We are made in the image of God, created with the purpose of God, waiting to be released.

I believe the timeless quote from Ecclesiastes: "There is a time for everything" is indicative of the simple truth that God has designed creation and everything in it, including man, for a specific purpose. However, before man can reach that end or that "season" there must be a process of growth, development, preparation and finally, release.

The definition of "process" offered by Webster's Dictionary is noteworthy as it adds insight to our discussion of this vital but often missed principle of process. Webster defines "process" as "1.) course, 2.) a series of changes leading to some result, 3.) a series of operations, as in manufacturing."

All of creation certainly is on a course toward destiny. A fruit seed produces a plant that is on a course to becoming a fruit-producing tree. Man is on a course to becoming who he was created to be, a replica of his Father God, able to function like God and fulfill his purpose, which is to dominate the earth.

A baby lion is born looking as harmless as a kitten, but through a series of changes or stages of growth, he eventually becomes the strong, majestic, intimidating creature referred to as the "king of the jungle."

In the same way, God allows us to be born as babies, but with the potential to become leaders, great men and women of faith and exploits. However, He allows us to go through the process of purpose, which is the process of God. Because God sees the end-product called fulfillment of purpose, He designs (or allows us to design by our adversary) the circumstances that will enable us to be prepared for each phase of our purpose.

This process can be likened to the work of a sculptor. The sculptor starts with a picture of the finished product in his or her mind and proceeds to shape and mold until they see the piece of art they had envisioned.

What is interesting about this process is that if one was to observe the piece of art in the process it might not make very much sense and in fact one might conclude that the sculptor is wasting their time.

I believe that many times we don't have an appreciation for what God is doing in our lives and the lives of others because we don't have a picture of the end product. In fact, people have given up and taken their own lives because they did not understand God had a plan for their lives. They didn't realize that the present process was not the end of that phase of their purpose.

Throughout this book, we're going to examine, gain insight and learn principles from the life of Jesus and other heroes of the faith such as Abraham, Moses, Joshua and others.

We will study what I call the "Seven Pillars of Process."

Pillar #1: "Process" is the Designer's suit for purpose.

There is no experience like arriving at your destination unprepared for the occasion. It nullifies the reason for your presence.

It cancels your opportunity to take advantage of the moment. Without the suit of process, you are bare and unprepared for your destiny. Had David arrived at his purpose with Goliath without his suit of process, he would have been mincemeat for Goliath.

Pillar #2: "Process" is the pathway to purpose

To every destination there is a definite pathway. The journey to the different phases of our purpose is no different. It is important to note that Jesus Himself followed a definite route to His different phases of purpose. In His phase of submission to authority, He submitted to His parents and allowed John to baptize Him. In His preparation for ministry phase, He allowed Satan to tempt Him. In His final phase of redemption, He submitted to injustices of a kangaroo court. Sometimes our pathway is certainly not the most pleasant, but it is necessary to enable us to arrive at our destination.

Pillar #3: "Process" is the plan of God for purpose

As we experience life and examine the Bible, it becomes increasingly clear that God's plan for fulfillment of purpose is "process." The flowers, the animals and man himself is evidence of this truth. As referred to in the second pillar, Christ Himself is proof of this plan. Usually when a tree does not complete the process of growth, it is referred to as being stunted. If a person does not complete their growth process, they are referred to as a midget or dwarf.

Lack of the completion of the process is easily recognizable. From a natural perspective, all of David's brothers seemed more likely to be kingly material; however, it was David who was chosen. Process is God's plan.

Pillar #4: "Process" prepares you for purpose

In the mind of Moses, he was ready from the day he tried to part the fight between his kinsman, but God was not of the same persuasion. When Moses returned from his preparation process, he was ready. I feel certain he had no idea of the kind of experience he was about to undergo. However, he was able to endure because he had submitted to the process.

Pillar #5: "Process" is the bridge from potential to purpose

Because we are made in God's image, we have tremendous potential inside us. The reason for the deposit of potential is to enable us to be prepared for our phases of purpose. The bridge that will take us from the shores of potential to our destinations of purpose is process. Process is the Refiner's fire for potential. Potential without process is wasted. Potential without process can be self-destructive and is similar to talent without character.

Pillar #6: "Process" provides for purpose

Joshua was trained in the process during his journey through the wilderness. It was that process that gave Joshua the ability to possess the land. It was the process of preparation that enabled the disciples to complete their purpose. The process provides for the future. Without the provision of the process, your purpose will never be fulfilled.

Pillar #7: Process is a result of purpose

Inherent in our purpose is the end result of our existence. Because of this truth, process becomes important because it enables us to achieve our purpose. Without purpose, there would not be a need for process.

God has destined us for greatness, but He also has designed the system to enable us to fulfill our purpose. This method is the process of purpose. There is no omitting the process and arriving at purpose. Potential without process is electricity without a conductor. Submission to the process results in fulfillment of purpose.

Chapter 1
PROCESS IS DESIGNED FOR PURPOSE

"It is not for man to rest in absolute contentment. He is born to hopes aspirations as the sparks fly upward, unless he has brutified his nature and quenched the spirit of immortality which is his portion."

--Robert Southey

"GOD IS A GOD OF PURPOSE, PLANS AND PROCESS"

All of us at one point or another have probably seen the beginning of the construction of a building. First, stakes are put into the ground and the next thing we see is a tractor digging a hole. Sometimes the hole is deeper than others and we wonder why are they digging such a deep hole. However, as the building process progresses and we see the huge structure taking shape, we realize that the depth of the hole was a necessity because of the size of the structure. The process of the construction was related to the purpose of the building.

As I already noted, Webster defines "process" as a course, or a series of changes leading to some result. Throughout this discussion of the process of purpose, when we expound on process, we will be referring to the dynamic series of experiences, circumstances, phases, or changes that God uses to impact our lives and to enable us to be in a position to maximize our potential and fulfill our purpose.

This metamorphosis relates to all areas of life: career, family, business, education and ministry. I am convinced that God is a God of purpose, plans and process.

Genesis is the book of beginnings and throughout creation we see God using the principle of process. Life itself is a process and if we can internalize this truth, we would have less difficulty with the challenges of life. Society is void of an understanding of this principle that is so evident in our stressful society.

Our pressured society is further affected by the instant gratification mentality we have developed because of technology. We feel that since our cereal is instant, our relationships should be instant and solutions to life's problems should be instant. Understanding the process of God will cause us to approach life differently. We'll begin to approach life with expectancy, optimism and faith.

In Genesis we see God beginning and completing creation using a systematic process of **preparation for purpose**. For example, we see the Garden of Eden being created before man was created because the Garden would be necessary to sustain him.

You see, life itself is a process. It's a physical process—none of us were born the size we are now. We started as infants and over the years have grown to our current size. God in His wisdom knew we needed time to develop size, strength and ability.

Life is also a process materially. Even though a pre-fabricated home can be built almost overnight a process was still necessary because the material still had to be manufactured.

Spiritually, life is a process–and that's where we lose it as believers.

Let's take a look at the life of Abraham for some of the process of God in this man's life. I'm not going to focus particularly on his faults, we know he was human just like us and we know he made mistakes. Instead, I want us to look at some of the positive aspects of the process of God in Abraham.

Interestingly, we're going to pick up the story of Abraham when he was about eighty years old. Perhaps it says something about the fact that you're never through with God and God is never through with you. I've got good news for those of you who are in your sixties and seventies: the world may say you're "finished," but God disagrees. Your productive years are not finished at the retirement age of sixty-five. In fact, you now have such a wealth of knowledge and experience that you can make a contribution to society by giving back some of what you received!

Abraham is a very appropriate person to study for this because through him God started a new nation. Abraham was to be the father of a whole new spiritual people. In Genesis 12 we learn that Abraham was chosen by God. It's interesting that when he was chosen by God, he had not gone through the process that we're going to look at now, yet God chose him.

Could it be that God chooses people who have not yet gone through the process, but who He wants to take through a process? God gives us the option to decide to be chosen or not to be chosen. He leaves that decision to us.

Genesis 12:1-4 tells us: "The Lord had said to Abram, 'Leave your country, your people and your father's household and go to the land I will show you. I will make you into a great nation and I will bless you; I will make your name great, and you will be a blessing.

"I will bless those who bless you, and whoever curses you I will curse; and all peoples on earth will be blessed through you. So Abram left, as the Lord had told him; and Lot went with him. Abram was seventy-five years old when he set out from Haran."

In this passage we see Abram going along, minding his own business so to speak, quite content with what he was doing, quite involved in what he was doing, and God comes along and says, "Abram, get out of your homeland. Get away from your kin, your family and leave your father's house. Go to a land that I will show you."

As I considered this passage I began to fully understand and appreciate what faith really is. I think some of what we call faith really isn't faith at all. We have such good examples of people who have exercised their faith. Abram, on the other hand, had few examples, if any. He did not have an entire Bible to read and study and gain inspiration from. His faith was based on simple obedience.

God came to him and told him to leave, plain and simple, and Abram did what he was told. Some of us are not at all willing to even consider going through the process of God because we don't want to leave our security.

This passage of Scripture, this Word that God gave to Abram is an awesome Word. In essence God was telling to leave all of his familiar surroundings; all of the things he had there, all of his security symbols, and go to a land that He would show him.

God doesn't even tell Abram very much about the land, He just says, "Go to a land that I will show you, and I will bless you, I will make your name great and I will make you a blessing." Abraham earned the designation of "Father of the faithful" by virtue of his obedience.

Abraham believed for things he had never seen before, that had never ever happened. I want you to understand something about his believing. If you're going to believe God for things that never ever happened, you're going to have to get rid of all of your security symbols.

Some of us believe only in the system that we know of—the world's system, the world's way of doing things. That's all we believe. If we're going to do what has never been done before, we're going to have to start believing that God can take us away from all of our security symbols and provide for us in ways we've never seen before.

Abraham didn't see anything, he didn't feel anything, it hadn't happened before. But he believed simply because God said so, that was enough for him. All Abraham had—to believe that he would be blessed—was simply the promise of God. You see, God has a way of reducing us to just Him and us.

I want you to notice something here about Abraham's obedience. It is usually based on three factors. First, we can be obedient out of respect. You know, your boss is your boss, right? He or she is over you and tells you what to do and out of respect for the office of the boss, you do it. That's one kind of obeying, and one reason to obey.

Secondly, we can obey out of fear. A parent tells their child to do something and the child obeys. Is it out of respect? No, the child obeys out of fear of punishment. Employees obey out of fear of losing their job.

Thirdly, however, is the reason I believe Abraham obeyed God. We can obey out of trust. Obeying out of trust is totally different from the other two because obeying out of trust has to do with obeying out of a relationship. Abraham didn't obey God because he was frightened and he didn't obey God simply because he respected God, although I'm sure he did. Abraham obeyed God out of trust because of his relationship with Him.

That's the kind of obedience God wants. God does not want us to obey Him simply out of fear. Unfortunately, for some of us, that's what we've been taught in church.

Genesis 12:7-8 says, "The Lord appeared to Abram and said, 'To your offspring I will give this land.' So he built an altar there to the Lord, who had appeared to him." An altar besides being a place of sacrifice was also one of the outward expressions of a person's trust in God. Throughout the Old Testament, whenever God said something or did something significant, the people stopped and built an altar. By building the altar to God they were saying that they trusted Him and were marking it right then and there.

I want to say something here about the covenant. In Genesis 12:2, God says, "*I will make you into a great nation and I will bless you; I will make your name great, and you will be a blessing. I will bless those who bless you, and whoever curses you I will curse; and all peoples on earth will be blessed through you."*

And then in Genesis 17:1-7 it says, "And when Abram was ninety-nine years old, the Lord appeared to him and said, 'I am God Almighty; walk before me and be blameless. I will confirm my covenant between me and you and will greatly increase your numbers.' Abram fell face-down, and God said to him, 'As for me, this is my covenant with you: You will be the father of many nations.

"No longer will you be called Abram; your name will be Abraham, for I have made you a father of many nations. I will make you very fruitful; I will make nations of you, and kings will come from you. I will establish my covenant as an everlasting covenant between me and you and your descendants after you for the generations to come, to be your God and the God of your descendants after you."

God calls Abram and then we see Him make a covenant with him. We know that broadly a covenant is a legal contract, but there is something interesting about a covenant. A covenant was always made between a greater party and a lesser party. In other words, in a covenant one party who was offering something to the other party. In this case, God was offering Abram to become a father of many nations, to be blessed, and for his children to be blessed after him.

God makes the same covenant with us. What do you think communion is all about? The wine we drink is symbolic of the blood of Christ that was shed when God decided to make a covenant through Jesus with mankind. The covenant is this: if you will accept Christ, I will give you life.

We don't have anything to bring to it, but our life. Abram had nothing to bring to their agreement, but his obedience. God was the One doing all of the offering. We don't bring anything to God, but our lives–as they are–and usually they're in a mess. He's doing all the offering.

God says, "I'll take away your heart of stone and give you a heart of flesh. I'll take away those old desires that were unprofitable and destructive and I'll place new desires inside of you for life. I will give you My Spirit to remind you of My Word. I will give you My Word to cause you to effect change in your world."

Although God came to Abram and said, "Leave your security," what He offered could not compare with anything Abram had.

Some of us have missed the riches of God because we have decided to hold onto dust. "God," you say, "I want my old desires, my old friends, and my old support systems. God I can't leave all that." You're holding onto dust, you're holding onto rags. You're robbing yourself of riches by holding onto rags. God, when He redeemed us, gave us access through the covenant to real riches.

In case you thought God came to Abram, said these things and just kind of walked away, Genesis 13:1-2 gives us evidence to the contrary: "*So Abram went up from Egypt to the Negev, with his wife and everything he had, and Lot went with him. Abram had become very wealthy in livestock and in silver and gold.*"

You see, when God makes a covenant, He confirms it through the process of God. If you ever attempt to avoid the process, you're in trouble. You'll miss it for every time.

There is a process in God. If we will become involved in the process of knowing, loving, and obeying God, we will experience benefits of the process. For Abraham, the gold and silver were simply what God threw in as benefits of the process. What God was after in the process was a relationship. Once the relationship gets established, some things come along with the package.

Jesus expounded this truth in Matthew 6:33 when He tells us to "*seek first his kingdom and his righteousness, and all these things will be given to you.*"

Let's look at what happens in Genesis 13:8 when God has a chance to work a process in us. "*So Abram said to Lot, 'Let's not have any quarreling between you and me, or between your herdsmen and mine, for we are brothers. Is not the whole land before you? Let's part company. If you go to the left, I'll go to the right; if you go to the right, I'll go to the left.'*"

Do you realize the seriousness of what Abram did? He was totally unselfish because of the process. You can be this unselfish only when you have a relationship with the Source. You see, through the process of God, Abram got to have such a relationship with God that he knew it didn't matter what land God promised him. He would prosper whatever land he went to.

We need to come to a point in our lives, in our walk with the Lord, when we can say, "God, whatever You say is fine because I know You well enough that You can prosper me in the midst of any circumstances." There's a blessing in the midst of the process of knowing and obeying God.

Consider Moses and his willingness to go back to Pharaoh. Moses knew how powerful Pharaoh was–he had experienced that power. But he had to be willing to go right in there, with all that knowledge about Pharaoh. He had to submit that knowledge, to his knowledge about God.

It's a matter of confidence. Perhaps some of us have our confidence in the land, rather than in God. Abram's confidence was not in the land, it was in the One who could make the land produce. Our confidence has to be in God.

I want you to contrast that with Lot. Lot looked around and did just what some of us would have done. He chose the land that "looked" fertile because his confidence was in the land.

The second result of the process, besides unselfishness, was Abram's courage. All throughout this book you're going to see another result of the process. You're going to see love in action; the kind of love that can only come from a process, from a relationship with God.

After Lot had taken the choicest land he got himself in trouble, but look what Abram does in Genesis 14:11, "*The four kings seized all the goods of Sodom and Gomorrah and all their food; then they went away. They also carried off Abram's nephew Lot and his possessions, since he was living in Sodom. One who had escaped came and reported this to Abram the Hebrew. Now Abram was living near the great trees of Mamre the Amorite, a brother of Eshcol and Aner, all of whom were allied with Abram.*

> "When Abram heard that his relative had been taken captive, he called out the 318 trained men born in his household and went in pursuit as far as Dan. During the night Abram divided his men to attack them and he routed them, pursuing them as far as Hobah, north of Damascus. He recovered all the goods and brought back his relative Lot and his possessions, together with the women and the other people."

What made Abram think he could take three hundred and eighteen soldiers and go against four kings? The only reason you would attempt that is if you've been through the process of God. You've gotten to the point in your relationship with God and you know Him so well that you know He will deliver you.

It would appear that as soon as Abram got the word he took action, he didn't even think about it because of his relationship with God. You cannot experience the depths of God's love and power without going through the process. There is no shortcut to success in God.

It's the same kind of process of God that David went through. David was called when he was young and he went through the process a long time because God was preparing David for his purpose. Many times the process involves situations and experiences that may seem insignificant at the time.

In David's case, one day along came a lion. David was going through the process and he killed the lion. One day there came a bear, and David was going through the process and he killed the bear.

We wonder sometimes why, when the adversary comes against us, we are so frightened. I believe many times we're bypassing the process. The process is interesting. Often, you are not in the spotlight when you are going through it. Many times it has to do with just you and God and no one else.

But there then comes a time when everyone will see, because the lion and the bear are coming and your confession will not deter them. If the lion and the bear had come along and David hadn't been going through the process, you never would have heard of David and Goliath. If you want to fulfill your purpose in God, you must submit to the process.

> *In Genesis 14: 20 Abram comes back from the battle with all the spoil: "And blessed be God Most High, who delivered your enemies into your hand. Then Abram gave him a tenth of everything." Look how benevolent he is, the first tithe. Abram gave a tithe out of knowledge of his Source. I am convinced that Christians who have a difficulty with tithing don't know the Source.*

> *Verse 21 continues, "The king of Sodom said to Abram, 'Give me the people and keep the goods for yourself.' But Abram said to the king of Sodom, 'I have raised my hand to the Lord, God Most High, Creator of heaven and earth, and have taken an oath that I will accept nothing belonging to you, not even a thread or the thong of a sandal, so that you will never be able to say, 'I made Abram rich.'"*

Another benefit of the process was Abraham's inability to be corrupted. You could not corrupt Abram. He was not impressed with goods. Abram had the kind of integrity we all need to develop. It came out of the process.

We live in such a materialistic society that we don't understood what riches are for. Even as Christians, our minds need to be renewed. Wealth is to be used for the kingdom. Personally, I'm not impressed with money; you don't move me because you've got a million dollars. I know my Source and He will bless me if I continue to obey His Word.

> *Jumping ahead to Genesis 18:23, Abraham has an interesting exchange with God: "Then Abraham approached him and said, 'Will you sweep away the righteous with the wicked? What if there are fifty righteous people in the city? Will you really sweep it away and not spare the place for the sake of the fifty righteous people in it?'"*

Abraham continues to bargain, boldly. How many of us would go to God like that? How many of us know Him that well to stand in His face and say, "God, now I know I came a moment ago, but what about thirty? Forty? Twenty? Ten?"

Obviously this man had gone through a process and he knew God. He knew God was just, so he knew he could go to God and talk to God about His justness. He knew something about the nature of God.

God had given him His heart of compassion for people. He didn't go and bargain for himself. This was a totally unselfish act, totally an act of love and concern for some other people not himself. If you will allow God to work in your life, He will take your heart of stone and give you a heart of flesh.

Some twenty years later, in Genesis 21:1,5, God fulfills a promise to Abraham: *"Now the Lord was gracious to Sarah as he had said, and the Lord did for Sarah what he had promised. Sarah became pregnant and bore a son to Abraham in his old age, at the very time God had promised him...Abraham was a hundred years."*

It was twenty years after the promise had been given and the covenant had been made. Why twenty years later? Why didn't God do it earlier? Because of the process of God. There were some things He wanted to put into Abraham that were not there twenty years before, so God decided to wait twenty years.

God's ability to do it was not a problem; He could have done it the next day. Why wait 20 years later, God? Because God had a process for Abraham to go through.

Why didn't He say to Moses, when Moses had an obvious concern for his people, when he killed the Egyptian, "Alright, Moses, I see you've got a concern, you want to set them free, let's go." No, there was a process Moses could not bypass.

I'm saying to you today, there's a process in your life you cannot bypass if you want to fulfill the will of God in your life. You cannot bypass the process because the lion and the bear are coming. But more so, the purpose and the plan of God require that you fulfill the process. If you bypass it, you can't fulfill the plan of God.

As I said before, I'm not focusing on the flaws in Abraham's character. We need to remember when we are reading the Bible that these men and women of God were just like us, imperfect humans. They were flesh and blood, but God chose them despite their human-ness just as He chooses you.

God never had a perfect man or perfect woman to do His will. He always chose men and women who could sin, who could miss Him, who could mess up. I say "Thank God" or none of us would qualify.

> Genesis 22:1-2 gives us another benefit of the process: God's test: "Some time later God tested Abraham. He said to him, 'Abraham!' 'Here I am,' he replied. Then God said, 'Take your son, your only son, Isaac, whom you love, and go to the region of Moriah. Sacrifice him there as a burnt offering on one of the mountains I will tell you about.'

I believe there comes a time, many times really, in the process of God where He gives us an opportunity to test ourselves. God knows beginning from end. He knew exactly what Abraham was going to do. The test was not for God, the test was for Abraham–to prove to himself how well he had done in the process of God. God also wanted to show him how much he had learned in trusting Him and how much he loved Him.

You could not shake him after that. He had proven it for himself. He had taken his son up, in his mind he had given him up; he had proven to himself that he loved God more than life itself. There are times in the process of God that He will give us opportunity to prove to ourselves where we're at. Sometimes we think we are where we're not.

The Gospels give an account of a rich man who thought he wanted God. In essence, Jesus said, "You really want Me? You really think you're at the point where you want Me? Above your security? OK, fine, take what you have and sell it, give the proceeds to the poor and come follow Me." The rich young ruler found out for himself that he was not where he thought he was.

Some people use that passage to prove that God doesn't want you to have any money, nonsense. The point is, Jesus wanted him to find out where he was, and he was not where he thought. He thought he was at the point where he wanted God more than anything else. The Bible says he went away sorrowful.

You know, it's possible he went away sorrowful because he realized, "God, I don't want You that much. O God." It's possible he realized, "God, I thought I wanted You, but I really don't want You all that much after all."

If you are going to do what God has called you to do, you cannot bypass the process of God. The work is too awesome, God's plan and purpose for your life is too big. Say to God, "God, let's go. Let's go through the process because I know what You're going to teach me. I know what You're going to do in my character. I know what You're going to do in my mind. I know what You're going to do with my lifestyle. Let's go God, let's go through the process. Because it's in the process of that relationship, God, I will get to know You, not just know about You."

It's alright to know whose you are, but it's better to know Him. See, it's fine to know, "I belong to God." That's great, but do you know God?

PROCESS POINTS

- In Genesis God used a systematic process of Preparation for purpose.

- Abraham obeyed God out of trust because of his relationship with God.

- When you become involved in the process of knowing, loving and obeying God, you will experience benefits of the process.

- The blessing is in the midst of the process of knowing and obeying God.

- You cannot experience the depths of God's love and power without the process of God.

- There are no shortcuts to success in God.

- Many times the process involves situations and experiences that seem insignificant at the time.

- There comes a time in the process of God when He gives you an opportunity to test yourself.

Chapter 2

PROCESS AND THE EFFECT OF YOUR ENVIRONMENT

"God asks no man whether he will accept life. That is not the choice. You must take it. The only choice is how."

--Henry Ward Beecher

"YOUR ENVIRONMENT WILL DETERMINE THE EXTENT TO WHICH YOU FULFILL YOUR POTENTIAL AND COMPLETE THE PROCESS OF PURPOSE"

We can learn a lesson about process from the seed. Inside the seed is a promise of a tree, and the seed has the potential of growth through the process. Without the process of growth, there can be no fruit, there can be no tree, and if there's no tree, there's no fruit. So we learned that the process is essential.

We do not understand all of the why's and how's of a seed growing. All we know is that if we put it in the ground under certain conditions, it will grow.

Likewise, we do not understand fully how the Word of God works. But we understand enough to know that if we apply the Word of God it will work under certain conditions. A seed has a destined end. Already inside the seed is an end that has been determined by the type seed. For example, inherent in an orange seed is an orange tree, not a mango tree.

Even as that seed, by its very nature, has an end result already destined in it, so the Word of God has an end already purposed in it. That's why, when God speaks, He speaks from a point of view of already knowing the end of what He's saying. He already knows the end of the process. He knows that inside the Word He's speaking, is the ability to bring it all to pass. That's why God can say to us, "Let the weak say I am strong." The weak may be weak, but God knows that in His Word is the ability to make the weak strong.

Likewise, He's not saying they're not weak. That's just worldly positive thinking. God is speaking from the point of view that although in the present they may be weak, by the time the Word completes its purpose they will be strong. So He says, "Let the weak say I am strong."

God speaks based on what He knows the Word has the ability to do and to produce at the end of the process. That's why we live by faith because we cannot afford to live on just what we know and see now. We have to be able to believe God for what we do not yet see. We have to be able to believe with God for the end result of the Word. We cannot allow ourselves to come to the place where we forget that the manifestation of the Word is a process and every process has an end, every seed has a fruit.

In the same way that we can believe in the natural for a crop, we need to be able to believe in the spiritual. We've got to be able to believe that despite what the situation is now, since the One who has the ability to make what He said come to pass has spoken, it will be a reality.

When Joshua and the army came to Jericho and God told them to walk around there once a day for six days, and then on the seventh day to go seven times, they had to be able to believe, because all they saw was wall.

That's the way it is in life, in the situations and circumstances that we face. All we can see sometimes is the situation; all you can see is the wall. The Israelites had never heard of a wall coming down by simply marching around it. This was not a repeat performance; they did not have anyone on record who did this before. Real faith has no other reason than that God said. They somehow had to believe that because God said to march around this thing, something was going to happen.

Matthew 13:1-17 says, "That same day Jesus went out of the house and sat by the lake. Such large crowds gathered around him that he got into a boat and sat in it, while all the people stood on the shore. Then he told them many things in parables, saying, 'A farmer went out to sow his seed. As he was scattering the seed, some fell along the path, and the birds came and ate it up. Some fell on rocky places, where it did not have much soil. It sprang up quickly, because the soil was shallow. But when the sun came up, the plants were scorched, and they withered because they had no root.

"Other seed fell among thorns, which grew up and choked the plants. Still other seed fell on good soil, where it produced a crop—a hundred, sixty or thirty times what was sown. He who has ears, let him hear. The disciples came to him and asked, 'Why do you speak to the people in parables?'

"He replied, 'The knowledge of the secrets of the kingdom of heaven has been given to you, but not to them. Whoever has will be given more, and he will have an abundance. Whoever does not have, even what he has will be taken from him. This is why I speak to them in parables: Though seeing, they do not see; Though hearing, they do not hear or understand. In them is fulfilled the prophecy of Isaiah: You will be ever hearing but never understanding; you will be ever seeing but never perceiving.

"For this people's heart has become calloused; they hardly hear with their ears, and they have closed their eyes. Otherwise they might see with their eyes, hear with their ears, understand with their hearts, and

turn, and I would heal them. But blessed are your eyes because they see, and your ears because they hear. For I tell you the truth, many prophets and righteous men longed to see what you see but did not see it, and to hear what you hear but did not hear it." Jesus goes on to explain what the parable means.

Why is the environment so important as it relates to the process of God? Your environment can determine and will determine the extent to which the full potential of the Word is released in your life. It will affect the process of the Word. Just as the environment for the seed will affect the potential of that seed to produce a tree.

Remember, all of the potential of the seed is wrapped up in the seed. All of the potential of the Word is in the Word, but your environment will determine how much of that potential is released.

The seed only produces its full potential under certain conditions. Take a seed and place it on the concrete and it will remain just a seed. No potential will come out of that. Why? The environment is not conducive to the potential of the seed coming forth. The environment is not right.

Webster's Dictionary defines "environment" like this: *"it's the circumstances, objects or conditions by which one is surrounded; the complex of physical, chemical and biotic factors that act upon an organism or an ecological community, and ultimately determine it's form and survival."* It's the last piece I really like: the conditions that act upon an organism which ultimately determine its form and survival.

Under certain conditions, a tree will come up in a certain way. You've seen trees that are stunted; they never came into full maturity. Or, they grow up and produce blossoms, but no fruit. Or, they produce blossoms and fruit, but never grew into full maturity and eventually drop over and die. Or, the tree grows into full maturity with blossoms and fruit, but when you bite into the fruit–it's not good at all.

Think about all the different forms a tree can come in, other than coming to full maturity after you have spent a lot of money on expensive fertilizer. Think about the Word and your environment and perhaps you can understand why the Word doesn't mature in certain situations.

The Word has in it the potential to produce but yet, in certain situations, it doesn't produce. The first response is to blame the Word, but you never stop to look at the environment. In order for the process to go to completion, you have to protect, and pay attention to, and insure that the environment is appropriate for the Word to produce.

There are some environmental factors we need to consider. First, there are factors in the environment that will swallow and devour the Word until there is no trace of it. You receive some of God's Word and when you find yourself in a situation where you need to activate the Word of God, there are factors waiting to totally thwart you. There are situations out there waiting, there are some set-ups the enemy has waiting or there are some environments which, if you are not careful, will totally devour that Word until there is no trace of it.

Have you ever known people who were excited about God and then all of a sudden they lose total interest? It's as if they never heard or read the Word. They have themselves in an environment that has totally eaten up the Word until there is no trace of them having ever received the Word. And you wonder, did that person ever hear what I heard? It's the environment that they have placed themselves in. That's due to their lack of understanding of the need to go through this process.

As kingdom citizens we have a responsibility to protect, pay attention to, and control our environment if we want the Word that is in us to go through the process to completion. It's like Noah and the ark. Do you realize it took him one hundred and twenty years to build that ark? It wasn't an overnight, instant situation.

Noah had a lot of opportunity, if he was not careful, to allow the environment to swallow the Word given him by God. I am sure people were continually questioning him on what he was doing. I imagine Noah talked to his sons everyday, reminding them of what God had said, "The Lord said, 'Build an ark,' let's build this ark, boys. Let's build it."

I believe he had to continually remind them of their mission because of the environment. I believe he made sure they didn't spend too much time around their friends, because their friends were probably doubting their entire project. So for one hundred and twenty years Noah had to protect his environment. When God calls you and gives you a vision, you need to be prepared to go through the process.

Finally, after one hundred and twenty years, the One who spoke it brought it to pass. He always does. But in the midst of the process, you've got to protect your environment. See, the environment is not going to allow you to go through the process.

Like Noah, you cannot always remove yourself from the environment. Fortunately, most times we can, but think about Noah again, he couldn't. At least we have the ability, most of the time, to control our environment, to determine what kind of people we associate with, to determine what kind of thoughts we think about. If we know that a particular environment won't help us fulfill our purpose, we can leave. If there is a particular environment at your job, maybe you can request a transfer. (Unless you need to go in the lunch room and start talking about the Lord!)

The first factor we see is that if we're not careful, there are things in our environment that will try to eradicate the Word from us. The adversary will send situations to try and get us to stop believing.

Secondly, there are factors that will make it very difficult for the Word to grow, thus growth is retarded. For example, you find yourself in an environment where you are kept away from the body of Christ. Maybe someone said something you didn't like or they did something that offended you or someone looked at you a certain way.

As a result you've decided, "I'm just going to stay home and receive the Word from television." Or, maybe you messed up and allowed the enemy to take advantage of a situation and now you're too ashamed to go back to church.

Whatever it is, any time you find yourself staying away from the body of Christ, you're going to affect the process of your growth. You are going to find that your growth will be stunted.

God has so designed the church, the body of Christ, that when we come together, something supernatural happens. First of all, by our very presence, we encourage each other, without even saying a word. Do you realize that when you walk in the church doors, and there are other believers there, you are automatically encouraged, just by their presence?

Secondly, when the Lord gives gifts to the church, it's for the entire church body, not just the individual to whom it was given. So when you come, you receive from the church body from the gift He gave the Body. And then the Body receives from the gift He gave you. So the body of Christ is built up.

God's Word says, "Iron sharpens iron, so a man, his brother." You can't sharpen iron if iron isn't in place. If it is not sharpened, it will stay dull.

If you disassociate yourself from the body, you're going to affect the process of your own growth because you are affecting your environment, and you are not making your environment conducive to growth. It will be hard and difficult for you to grow; it's going to be like the seed that fell among the rocks.

The seed that fell among the rocks will grow a little bit, but it's going to be stunted. In other words, it's going to look strange. I am sure you know people who seem to have reached a certain point in their spiritual walk and don't seem to grow any more. They have aborted the process.

Thirdly, there are factors in the environment that, if allowed to continue to exist, will eventually choke the Word. We call these factors compromise. In Matthew 13:7, "*Other seed fell among thorns, which grew up and choked the plants.*"

31

Any time thorns are growing up near your plants or flowers, you have two choices: pull them up or leave them there. If you leave them there, they're going to eventually fight your flowers for position, nourishment and sunshine. Thorns (of any type) are not interested in co-existing. Thorns are interested in taking over; they're not interested in peace. They're interested in dominating.

There may be situations in your life that you know you need to change because you are compromising your relationship with the Lord. Rest assured, those situations are not there to live peaceably with your relationship with God—it's war. That compromising situation is there to take over, and if allowed to exist, it's like the thorns.

The Holy Spirit's telling you, "Look, that's compromise, that's not in line with kingdom living. It might be OK as far as the world's standards are concerned, but it's not OK as far as kingdom lifestyle is concerned."

Sometimes this is how the adversary deceives us. There are a lot of things in the world that are permissible--it's how the world operates. In the world it's no problem. If you're not careful you may think it's permissible in the kingdom, even though the Holy Spirit is telling you it is not.

When you come to Christ and the Holy Spirit takes up residence, you don't have to wonder about right or wrong. Remember what Jesus said, "I'm going to put them on your heart now. My laws are going to be on your heart." How are they going to be on your heart? Because of the One who is inside of you. He's going to tell you if it's in line or not. You don't have to wonder. All the wondering is over with. The minute the Holy Spirit sees a situation that's compromise, He tells you.

The Holy Spirit is there to lead you into all truth. In order to do this, He obviously must identify untruths. He tells you right away, "Look, that's not in line with God's Word." You may think the Holy Spirit is there trying to take away some joy or rob you of something pleasurable. The Holy Spirit is actually protecting you; we just do not understand what the Holy Spirit is doing. He is there to protect you, because He has already seen the end result of the compromise.

The spirit of compromise is from the devil. He couldn't stop you from making your commitment to the Lord so the next best thing is to try and get you to compromise, get you to a place where you half-heartedly adhere to kingdom living.

Although the seed has in it the ability to bring us through the process, it is always affected by its environment. As we go through the process, we must protect our environment so that the Word can accomplish its purpose. Remember what we said in the beginning, the Word has in it a destined end–its purpose. If we do not protect our environment, the Word will never be able to accomplish its purpose because the process will be disrupted.

Jesus spoke about this in Matthew 13:13 parable because the average religious person would never understand the significance of what He was saying. So He said, "They'll hear, but they won't understand. They'll see, but they wouldn't see."

Jesus called these principles secrets because the unsaved do not care about the environment. To the unsaved person, anything goes. They are not concerned about their environment. Being a kingdom citizen necessitates protection of your environment. Some citizens never progress in the process of God because they do not control, nor do they protect their environment. They open themselves up to just about anything, anyone and any influence. The Word never has opportunity to come to fruition in their life.

Matthew 13:12 is interesting: "Whoever has will be given more, and he will have an abundance. Whoever does not have, even what he has will be taken from him." It sounds like a contradiction, doesn't it?

Jesus is saying that those who have, will be given more, but they who don't have, what they do have will be taken away from them. How could you take something if someone doesn't have anything?

Obviously what He's saying is, everyone has. The Bible says, "Everyone has been given a measure of faith," so we all have. But those who use what they have will be given more. Those who don't use the Word they already have, then the cares of this world, the rocky ground and their bad environment will take it away. What they have they lose; when they should in fact be gaining with what they have.

If you're not using what you have and producing more with it, what you have will be taken from you. Because you started out with a measure of faith, you started out with the same Word. The more he receives, the more he understands; the more he understands, the more he receives." And the more he receives, the more he understands; and the more he understands, the more he receives. He continues to grow.

Whoever does not protect their environment will lose the ability to receive more of the Word. It's only by protecting your environment do you receive more, and you understand more, and you receive more. If you don't protect it, you're going to lose the ability to receive more because you didn't understand and use what you already had.

> *Matthew 13:19 says, "When anyone hears the message about the kingdom and does not understand it, the evil one comes and snatches away what was sown in his heart. This is the seed sown along the path."*

Our environment determines whether or not we understand God's Word. Our environment cannot be filled with nonsense or people who are not interested in the Word. When the Word goes forth, you won't even understand it because your environment is so polluted that you cannot even understand what in the world is going on. It is difficult to see clearly in the midst of pollution.

Have you ever been so confused when someone shared something with you that even though it made sense, you still couldn't understand? If you don't protect your environment, you will come to the point where even when the Word is shared with you, you still won't understand what's going on because your environment has become so messed up.

Matthew 13:20-21 says, "The one who received the seed that fell on rocky places is the man who hears the word and at once receives it with joy. But since he has no root, he lasts only a short time. When trouble or persecution comes because of the word, he quickly falls away."

Why does he quickly fall away when trouble or persecution comes? His environment is such that he has not protected it. When trouble or persecution comes, instead of understanding that the one who spoke the Word will bring it to pass, instead of understanding that the Word has in it a destined end, and that if he will operate in faith, he will receive the end that the Word has in it, he instead gives up. He abandons the Word because he has not protected his environment and so the process is affected.

The environment determines whether or not we have root. When trouble and persecution comes, we should have our environment so rooted, so protected that the trouble and the persecution cannot in anyway stop the Word from working. It can't stop the process from continuing because we have protected our environment in such a way.

Abraham is a good example of that. Genesis 18:18-19 says, *"Abraham will surely become a great and powerful nation, and all nations on earth will be blessed through him. For I have chosen him, so that he will direct his children and his household after him to keep the way of the Lord by doing what is right and just, so that the Lord will bring about for Abraham what He has promised him."*

We could paraphrase that to say, "I (God) have chosen Abraham because he will so protect his environment that he will ensure that what I have spoken will come to pass." Why does it come to pass? Because he will protect his environment.

God's Word already has in it everything to accomplish what it's sent to do. But if we do not protect the environment, the Word will not have the opportunity to bring it to pass.

This passage also says, "He'll command his children and his household." In other words, when you came to work for Abraham, you had to straighten up and come in line with his rules. You were subject to his standards. Why was Abraham setting a standard for even his servants? This man understood that although God had promised him an inheritance, his servant could interfere with the process if he did not protect and control the environment.

There are standards Abraham had to set in order to protect his environment. Certain things just were not permissible in Abraham's house. Certain topics and conversations were not discussed in Abraham's house. Certain music was not played in Abraham's house.

Look what the Lord says about Abraham: "I've chosen him." Why? "*Because I know this man. He is going to so protect his environment that what I speak will be able to come to pass.*" What a tremendous example and testimony.

Process Points

- Without the process of growth, there can be no fruit.

- A Seed has a destined end.

- The word of God has an end that already has been purposed.

- Real faith has no other reason than the fact that God Said.

- In order for the process to go to completion, you have to protect, and pay attention to, and insure that the environment is appropriate.

- Compromise will choke the word of God.

- Being a kingdom citizen necessitates the protection of your environment.

The environment determines whether or not we have root.

Chapter 3

MAN'S RESPONSE: A KEY PRINCIPLE

"A will submitted to God transcends the impossibilities of life"

"ONE OF THE MOST PRECIOUS POSSESSIONS GOD HAS GIVEN US IS OUR WILL, BUT WITH A WILL COMES RESPONSIBILITY""

Once there was a man in need of food who prayed to God to provide for him. Soon, there was a knock on his door from a neighbor who brought him some seeds. He thanked the neighbor, put the seeds in a dish and each morning continued to pray for food. A week later, a friend came by. The man shared his plight and told him he was disappointed that God did not answer his prayer. The friend looked at the man and gently said, "God gave you the seeds, but you must plant them"

I believe this story describes the position we find ourselves in at times. We forget that our response to God is the key. The maturing process of God is a lifetime process. For the rest of our lives we will be maturing in God's process because there is so much in God.

It's great to read about God's responsibility. We love to hear what God will do for us and what we will receive. But as we read the Bible we start to see that we also have a part in the process of God. We have some responsibilities.

One of the most precious possessions God has given us is our will. With the will comes responsibility on how we will carry out our actions, hopes, desires, etc. Because God chose to give us a will, He will always give us responsibility so that we can put our will into use. Without responsibility, there is no opportunity to use your will. The dog does not have to exercise his will when it comes to barking, he has no choice. He can't talk, so he has to bark. But when it came to man, God chose to give us a will.

One of the first responsibilities we have is found in Philippians 2:12-18: *"Therefore my dear friends, as you have always obeyed— not only in my presence, but now much more in my absence—continue to work out your salvation with fear and trembling, for it is God who works in you to will and to act according to his good purpose."*

> *"Do everything without complaining or arguing, so that you may become blameless and pure, children of God without fault in a crooked and depraved generation, in which you shine like stars in the universe as you hold out the word of life–in order that I may boast on the day of Christ that I did not run or labor for nothing. But even if I'm being poured out like a drink offering on the sacrifice and service coming from your faith, I am glad and rejoice with all of you. So you too should be glad and rejoice with me."*

One of the first responsibilities we have in the process of God is to work out our own salvation.

There are two major things I see in this verse. First, this passage is not teaching that a saved or unsaved person can do good works to earn salvation. That's not what it means when it says, "Work out your salvation." Paul is addressing the church, the saints; he's talking to people who are already born again. The Bible is clear that we are not saved by any acts of righteousness.

Secondly, this passage is not implying that it is possible for us to work out and have a salvation that we ourselves work in. Salvation comes from God; it's His work and His alone.

Paul is telling us that we have the responsibility in the process of God, of working it out, not of working it in. The implication of the words "work out" in the Greek is that of working out a mathematics problem. Or, carrying something to its ultimate conclusion. Paul is saying that although you are born again, there is a process of you carrying out the fact that you're saved, the fact that you're born again. He's now talking about you carrying that fact to its ultimate conclusion, and the ultimate conclusion of your salvation is supposed to be you becoming more and more in the image and likeness of God.

After we accept Christ and become born again, we become a citizen of the kingdom of God. From that point on there is a process of us working out our salvation, working out the fact that we are in another kingdom and taking it to its ultimate conclusion.

In school if a math teacher gave you a problem and said, "Work out this problem." He or she is telling you to come up with the answer, to solve it. You solve it when you come up with the answer. You go to your desk and on paper try to work it out. If you come up with the wrong answer, you haven't "worked" the thing out. The teacher sends you back until you bring it to its proper conclusion.

Until we find ourselves totally in the image and likeness of God, we have not finished working out our salvation. However, it will take us a lifetime to work this out. Paul is saying, "Take the truth of your salvation, take all of the implications of what it means to be born again, and take it to its final conclusion."

Some people stop by simply writing down the sum. They simply described what the teacher said, write it down and say, "I'm finished, Teacher." They never go on to try and work the thing out. Paul is speaking here to the church, to the saints, and he's saying, "Work it out, take it to its final conclusion. Go through the process of it until you've got the thing worked out, and don't stop working it out."

It's going to take us a lifetime to complete the process. That's how vast the implications are of our salvation. We were done a disservice that they didn't explain to us when we accept Christ and came into the kingdom of God that we now have a lifetime process of working out the truth of that salvation. Some of us have thought that when we gave our life to God, that was it. Some people have the "make-it-in" mentality, they're satisfied just to make it in to the kingdom of God.

You know what happens if you have the make-it-in mentality? You make a commitment to God and then sit back and say, "Well, I did my part, I'm in. Now Lord, let all of the promises that are in the covenant just manifest in my life. I don't need to do anything else."

However, that's not the way growth takes place. It doesn't happen like that. We then start to ask God questions like, "Lord, how come You didn't do this? I read this in the Word that You said You'd do this. You say I'd be this and You say this would belong to me. Lord, how come this didn't happen?"

The irony of this is that these people then start to blame God! Can you believe that? God has given us a gift that is so vast in its scope, so broad in its implications that it takes us a lifetime to work out. And here we are, running back to God, blaming Him. I'm convinced God has a wonderful sense of humor from working with us!

If you walk away with the make-it-in mentality, you're headed for failure. God has not designed your growth process and purpose fulfillment to work if you are not actively involved in the process. God will not override your will no matter how sincere you may be in your erroneous thinking.

Paul is giving some responsibility now, in the process of God, to the church. He's telling us, "Work it out and carry it to its ultimate conclusion or its ultimate goal." As Paul prepares to leave these people, he says to them, "Work out your own salvation." In other words, your relationship with God is personal and I know while I was here I helped you in certain ways.

He's saying, "You have your own salvation from God. You have your own personal relationship with God; now work it out because I'm leaving. I won't be here any longer for you to call on, for you to get counsel from."

Paul sets before them their human responsibility and their growth in grace. He has their sanctification in mind; he's envisioning the whole process of them becoming like Christ. They are exhorted to carry it to its ultimate conclusion.

> In 1 John 3:2-3, it says, "Dear friends, now we are children of God, and what we will be has not yet been made known. But we know that when He appears, we shall be like him, for we shall see him as he is. Everyone who has this hope in him purifies himself, just as he is pure."

Everyone who has this hope purifies himself. It almost sounds like a contradiction because the next line says, "Even as he is pure." But it's not a contradiction; it's referring to the exact same thing Paul is talking about. Paul is saying, "You are born again. You are citizens of the kingdom, now work that truth out."

He's saying, "Everyone who has the hope of being like Christ works out his salvation and purifies himself, even as he is already in Christ he is already pure."

You see, the implication is the very same thing we're looking at here in the book of Philippians. In Philippians 2:12, Paul says, "*Therefore, my dear friends, as you have always obeyed—not only in my presence, but now much more in my absence—continue to work out your salvation with fear and trembling.*"

What is this "salvation" Paul is talking about? Well, in the very next verse he explains that, "for it is God who works in you to will and to act according to His good purpose." He's talking about God being allowed to work in us.

The fact that it is God who works in us is a very clear implication to me that we are allowing God to do us. We have to, as our human responsibility in this process, allow God to work in us.

We see two things here. First, God works in us according to our will. God gave us a will and He gives us responsibility to display our will. We are the ones who have to decide if we will allow God to work in us. That's a position we don't like to be in. We like God just to work in us. But our will has something to do with the working of God in us.

Secondly, the reality of your salvation is determined by your desire to change. Your human responsibility in the process has to do with your desire to change. What happens when people just want to make it in? They have no desire to change–God then has a difficult time working in them. He wants to work, He's waiting to work in them, but He can't do too much because their desire to change is not there.

It would be great if we could just lay back and say, "Lay it on, I made it in." We would love to have our growth in the Lord totally dependent on Him, but it doesn't work that way.

Because of the magnitude of our salvation, because of what God wants to do inside us, we have to give Him access with our will. The most precious gift you have from God is your will. With your will you determine how much of your responsibility you will take from God. Many times we make excuses for our limitations by blaming others. However, you determine how far you go in God.

God gives us His resources–He's so good! He gives us the precious resource of His Holy Spirit. Philippians 2:13 is a serious verse: "*for it is God who works in you to will and to act according to his good purpose.*" That's powerful!

God is obviously telling us, through Paul's writing, that we cannot even will without His help. You see how hard it is for people without God to do God's will? Without the Holy Spirit, we can't even will, according to His purpose. So He gives us His precious resource of the Holy Spirit to help us to do His good pleasure. As spiritual as we may think we are, we can't even have a desire to obey God without the Holy Spirit.

It is God who works in each of us. He gives us the responsibility, then He gives us His resources, and then He gives us the Holy Spirit.

In John 7:37-38 are some requirements for willing and doing God's good pleasure: *"On the last and greatest day of the Feast, Jesus stood and said in a loud voice, 'If anyone is thirsty, let him come to me and drink. Whoever believes in me, as the Scripture has said.'"*

We must become thirsty for the things of God. How thirsty are you? How much trust do you have in God? Have you been blaming God because things haven't been happening?

So the two requirements to us wanting God to will and to do in us is first of all, a thirst for God, and then a trust in God. Do you still trust in your own wisdom? Do you still trust in your own ability?

You don't have a desire for God just on your own. It is God who is constantly supplying the impulse, constantly giving you the desire for Himself, giving you both the power to resolve, and the strength to perform His good pleasure.

Thank God that He does not simply give us responsibility and walk away and say, "You handle it the best way you can." God is a just and fair God. He never asks you to do anything that He doesn't give you the ability to do. The problem is, sometimes when God asks us to do something, we get the impression He's telling us to do it without Him. We take off on our own and end up running into problems.

Philippians 2:14-16 says, "Do everything without complaining or arguing, so that you may become blameless and pure, children of God, without fault in a crooked and depraved generation, in which you shine like stars in the universe, as you hold out the word of life—in order that I may boast on the day of Christ that I did not run or labor for nothing."

Paul is saying to stop acting like babies–arguing and complaining about everything. Maybe you're not working out your salvation. Maybe you're still a baby and you're arguing and complaining about everything.

Could he also be saying that when we start to work out our salvation, we start to grow? It's possible that as we start to focus on other people's needs, our eyes come off of ourselves and we're not as important as we thought.

Philippians 2:14 says "*so that you may become blameless and pure.*" If we don't start taking our responsibility in the process some impurities will remain. God is saying we have impurities, "and a crooked and depraved generation in which you shine like stars in the universe." Look at what He's hoping for us to do. Look at what He's admonishing us to do. Look what happens if we start to work it out, we start to shine. Two things happen when we shine, we give light to those around us and we become an example.

If you have to look up in the sky and ask "Is that a star?" it must not be a star yet. The nature of stars is that they shine. Two things happen when we shine, we give light to those around us and we become an example.

Paul compares the citizen of the kingdom of God, who is working out the fact of their salvation, to a star. Such a citizen, like a star, will start to shine. There's something unique and special about stars–people notice them without the star ever trying to be noticed.

Now, you shine in two ways: you shine from the world and you shine for the world to see. How will the world know that there's a star to show them the way if you don't shine?

Why should you shine? Philippians 2:16 says, "*As you hold out the word of life.*" If you have no other reason for working out your salvation, if you have no other reason, Paul gives you a reason: to hold out the word of life.

Paul is saying that as a Christian, as a citizen of the kingdom, you have the Word of life. You have the potential, if you will, to give the Word of life to someone else.

Whether you give the Word of life to someone or not, is directly related to your working out your salvation. Have you given the Word of life to anyone lately? Perhaps it's because you are not shining. Perhaps it's because you're too busy arguing and complaining about everything. Perhaps it's because you have not submitted your will to God's will.

We know God is the One Who wants to will and to do. He sent the Holy Spirit to live inside of you, to insure that it happens. Our first responsibility in the process is to work out our salvation.

God, it would seem from His Word, has always desired a personal relationship with us. It seems very clear here, that God still wants a one-on-one where you relate to Him and He relates to you. He gives us His Holy Spirit, and the Holy Spirit says to us, let's work on this, this is His good pleasure here, let's do this.

Then He leaves it up to us to decide whether we're going to take our responsibility for the use of our will and say to the Holy Spirit, "Yes, let's do that." Because it's His good pleasure and that's what I want to do. We have a serious responsibility; we have the Word of life.

If we fail to work out our salvation, we can keep life from people. We could end up like the Scribes and the Pharisees if we don't give life. I want you to think about that a minute. Why did Jesus rebuke the Scribes and Pharisees? It was because of their hypocrisy, but the root of it all was their failure to give life.

They walked around with an outward form, but no life. That's serious. You usually call that a ghost. If you see clothes walking around with nobody inside, that's a ghost. The problem Jesus had with the Scribes and Pharisees was that they were walking around, wearing robes, sitting in high places, but not giving any life.

Graveyards are interesting places. They have plenty of bodies, but they don't give life. That's the seriousness of the predicament we could find ourselves in as citizens of the kingdom if we don't give life. We have to be responsible in working out our salvation, it's not an option. Either you work it out or be prepared to be a ghost.

We have in the process of God some tremendous responsibilities. First, to work out our salvation. My hope and prayer is that today you will begin to realize your responsibility in the process of God. Yes, God supplies the spiritual ability to go through the process, but He leaves some responsibility to us. As we respond to Him, He enables us to go through the process.

Paul's words to the church at Philippi are some very important words. In fact, those words affected the very future of the early church because if those saints had failed to take their responsibility in working out their salvation they could have actually caused the church to cease to exist.

Today I encourage you to make a fresh commitment to God, to work out your salvation. Don't sit back and assume He's going to do it and Christian growth will automatically happen to you.

No, God gives the responsibility to us. He waits with the ability to fulfill the responsibility that He's given us. Your fulfillment of your destiny in God is in your hands.

PROCESS POINTS

- One of the most precious possessions God has given us is our will.

- It will take us a lifetime to work out our salvation.

- God has given us a gift that is so vast in its scope, so broad in its implications, that it takes s a life time to work it out.

- God works in us according to our will.

- The reality of your salvation is determined by your desire to change.

- When we shine, we give light to those around us and we become an example.

- The failure of the scribes and pharisees was that they failed to give life.

Chapter 4
THE PROCESS OF
A RENEWED MIND

"As a man thinketh in his heart so is he" Proverbs 28:7

"THERE IS A PROCESS OF CONVERSION THAT DETERMINES YOUR ABILITY TO COMPLETE THE PROCESS"

One of the most important truths you will ever learn from the Bible is that God is a God of process. In Genesis God gave us a classic example of this truth. He took six days to create the world and everything in it. He could have done it in one, but He did it in six. I think He did it this way because He is a God of process and He wanted us to see and understand how He is and how He works.

In Chapter Two of this book we dealt with the fact that we have a responsibility to work out our own salvation according to Philippians 2. Working out our salvation does not mean we are able to affect our own salvation or that we are able to make our salvation a reality. Instead, it means that salvation is a fact.

God has given us the ability, through His Spirit, to cause the fact of our salvation to be a reality, a continual unfolding in our life. There is nothing whatsoever that we can do to cause our salvation to be a reality. We can't do any good works to earn it.

God has something in mind for us when He brings us into His kingdom. He does not bring us into the kingdom and say, "Amen, that's it." He has a goal in mind and He supplies the strength and the ability for us to make it a reality.

In this chapter we look at our second responsibility in the process of God: the renewing of our mind.

Matthew 22:36- is one of those occasions in the life of Jesus when the Pharisees thought that they would give Him a question He could not answer. *"Teacher, which is the greatest commandment in the Law? Jesus replied: 'Love the Lord your God with all your heart and with all your soul and with all your mind.'"*

Of course anytime God tells us to do something, it's because we would not do it automatically. Nowhere in the Bible do you see God saying to you, "Breathe." Why? You do it naturally; it's natural for you to breathe.

But He does tell us to "love the Lord your God with all of your mind" because He knows it's not something we would necessarily do naturally. It's something we have to make a conscious decision to do. You either do things one of two ways: you either do it consciously or unconsciously.

According to Webster's Dictionary the definition of the "mind"—and every so often he does have some good meanings—is *"the element or complex elements in an individual that feels, perceives, thinks, wills and reasons."* If our mind does all these things, I can understand why we're to love the Lord our God with all of our mind. The next definition says: "It is the organ; it is the organized conscious and unconscious adaptive mental activity of an organism."

The third definition is very interesting: *"Your mind is your intention or your desire."* Before we do anything we think about it. And we think about it in accordance to what we have heard about it. Either we read about it or someone told us something about it, but the information was passed onto us by someone or something.

Why as a youngster did you go to school? Because there were a number of things you did not know. Someone had to tell you. Somewhere along the way information was passed onto you.

Let's look at the definition for "renew": "to make like new, to make like new, to make new." Now, this next one is also in Webster's believe it or not: "To make new spiritually." He got revelation from somewhere!

The third definition is, "To restore to existence; to make extensive changes." I want you to think about these definitions in a minute. The word "restore" means "to return to an original state after depletion or loss." In order for us to really love the Lord with all of our mind, our minds have to be renewed as that of a citizen of the kingdom of God.

From the day we were born we have been receiving information from various sources–books, parents, family, television, teachers, neighbors, etc. We've been receiving information into our mind and that information has been determining our behavior.

This is where a lot of Christians lose it, right at this point. Even after they have given their lives to the Lord and are born again, their minds remain the same. Being born again is your spirit coming alive to the Spirit of God. You now have access to God, you now have access to His Spirit so you can understand the Word of God and it can affect your mind.

It's so important to realize that we have a responsibility in the process of God. Otherwise we'll continue as a citizen of this new kingdom and one day stand in bewilderment saying, "Well God, I gave my life to You. What's wrong with my mind? How come You're not dropping stuff on me? How come I'm not thinking right?"

There are a lot of Christians who are still not thinking right about a lot of things. Their thinking is not right, and you hear people say things like, "I can't believe he's a Christian. I can't believe she's a Christian." I can believe it because something is wrong with their mind. Perhaps they thought God was simply going to do what He did to their spirit, that He would miraculously change their mind. And all of a sudden they're going to think correctly. That would have been nice, but that's not the way it works. That's why we are told to renew our minds.

All He says to us about salvation is to receive it. He gives it, we receive it. If He was going to renew our mind for us, He would not have said anything. He would simply do it, and we would have had the benefit of it. But He leaves that as a part of our responsibility in the process of your salvation.

One of the most precious gifts God has given us, in fact the most precious thing God has ever given mankind, is the Word of God. That's why the enemy battles for your mind. Why do you think the enemy is so concerned about the media? Because it affects the mind, it affects your will. Once you've gotten the wrong information, you will make the wrong decision.

We need to be in the right place to receive the right information. Sometimes, even as citizens of the kingdom of God, we have friends in the kingdom we spend time with. Suddenly you find yourself wanting to do something that's not in line with the Word. You slack off. Why? Because you've made up your mind you want to do this thing and you don't want anyone telling you about God's Word.

If we want to make the right decisions, we should surround ourselves with people who are going to give us right information. It's not even enough to come and give your heart to the Lord and go back into the same environment. Why? You'll go back to getting wrong information.

You say, "But I'm now a Christian." Yes, but you'll get wrong information and make bad decisions. God always gives you the opportunity to take your will and submit it to Him.

There is a way that citizens of the kingdom of God are supposed to think. Let's examine Ephesians 4:19-24, "*Having lost all sensitivity, they have given themselves over to sensuality so as to indulge in every kind of impurity, with a continual lust for more. You, however, did not come to know Christ that way.*

> *"Surely you heard of him and were taught in him in accordance with the truth in him in accordance with the truth that is in Jesus. You were taught, with regard to your former way of life, to put off your old self, which is being corrupted by its deceitful desires; to be made new in the attitude of your minds; and to put on the new self, created to be like God in true righteousness and holiness"*

Once again Paul is telling us how to live godly lives. Why? Because we won't do it naturally. You will not naturally think the right thoughts; you have to make a conscious decision to do it. That's why it seems so hard at times. Sometimes you get thoughts and you're wrestling, it seems, and you say, "This seems so hard." Well, it's because it's not natural yet. But if you keep at it, just as you formed that old habit, if you will keep at this new way of thinking, if you will stay in the Word, you will come to a place where it becomes easier for you to think right because you've practiced it. It's becomes a part of your lifestyle now.

Paul tells us how the new man thinks with a renewed mind: "Wherefore, putting away lying," Lord, You mean to tell me the saints would lie? If the saints didn't do it, He wouldn't have to tell them to put it away. So the renewed mind does not lie, does not entertain lying thoughts. When you, as a citizen of the kingdom, are faced with situations where you have the opportunity to lie, pass them up.

You need to understand that speaking the truth to your neighbor sometimes puts you in an uncomfortable position. Sometimes you don't want to hurt people's feelings, you don't want to be rude, you don't want to seem like you don't care. Everyone wants to be nice, right? Someone once said, "It's more important to be right than to be nice."

We need to speak the truth in love. We need to use tact and ensure that we are not telling the truth with the wrong motive. Genuine love and concern should be our motive. The attitude and spirit in which the truth is told is as important as the truth which is being told. This requires a certain level of maturity because it requires you to believe that your brother or sister has your best interest at heart.

Otherwise, if someone tells you the truth and it sounds harsh, you may think, "Boy, they must not like me. Look what they said to my face." However, if you are at a certain level of maturity, you will instead think, "Boy, they must really love me because they're telling me, as hard as it seems. They'd rather see me be right than to go wrong. That response requires spiritual maturity.

How does the renewed mind think? Ephesians 4:26 says, "*In your anger do not sin.*" Sometimes people do things and we get angry. God is saying, "There isn't anything wrong with being angry, but in the expression of your anger, don't sin." It requires maturity because although you're angry, you've got to now stop and say, "God, I am angry as I can be, but how can I express this thing without sinning?"

Well, your mind has to be renewed. You're angry, upset and about to sin when you remember that God's Word says, "Love them." "Love those who do you wrong." "Don't return evil for evil, leave that to the Lord. Because evil has within it its own reward."

If someone has done you evil, inside of that evil is its own reward. It will take care of itself; they will receive what they have sown. Don't sin because you might reap something you didn't want. Even with a renewed mind you will still get angry at times–just don't sin.

What else does the renewed mind do? Verse 26 also says, "*Do not let the sun go down while you are still angry.*" That's the way the renewed mind thinks. You're upset at someone about something, but don't let a day pass without patching up things.

Verse 27 adds, "*and do not give the devil a foothold.*" Here is what we don't understand about an unrenewed mind. The unrenewed mind is fertile soil for the lies of the enemy. When you are not thinking in accordance with the Word of God, your mind becomes fertile soil for the enemy to plant his lies.

Instead, we can allow the truth of the God's Word to build up a wall, if you will, of protection. So when a lie of the enemy comes and hits against the wall, the Word of God says, "Be angry but sin not." Up goes the wall, you get angry, and the enemy says, "Look, man, you're angry. Sin!" But it hits the wall because there is some protection there. The truth is there because the thinking is right.

The enemy cannot have a field day with your mind. The King James Version words Ephesians 4:27 it this way: "nor give place to the devil." Do you realize that implicit in that verse is the fact that you can decide not to give place. I stated earlier that the most precious thing God has given us is a will. If it were not possible for you not to give place, it would be totally illogical and unfair for God to say to you, "nor give place to the enemy." But we miss our responsibility in the process of God because we've thought that God is going to do it all. Once I give my life to Him, I expect Him to do everything, and I just go about my business.

How do you give place to the devil? Verses 22-23 tell us, "*You were taught, with regard to your former way of life, to put off your old self, which is being corrupted by its deceitful desires; to be made new in the attitude of your minds.*"

You do not give place when you renew your mind. You do give the enemy place with the dumb thoughts that you yourself can't believe you were thinking.

Verse 28 says, "*He who has been stealing must steal no longer.*" Is God telling us that citizens of His kingdom, born-again believers could steal? That's exactly what God is saying. If your mind is not renewed, you could steal.

You want to see evidence of a renewed mind? Not just evidence of a changed life, of someone who has given their life to the Lord, but evidence of a renewed mind? Let the fellow who stole, stop stealing, go to work, and give to those who need. Then you will see someone who is renewing his mind.

If you are born again, healthy and hardy, and sitting in your momma's house all day long and eating off of her, you are stealing. Renew your mind. Show everybody it is renewed by getting a job and working with your hands. Before you were using your mother's hands, now work with your own hands. When you're on the job, don't steal your employer's goods—including his time. If he is paying you to work eight hours, don't work seven. If you do, you are still stealing.

How does a renewed mind think? What is our responsibility in the process? "Let no corrupt communication proceed out of your mouth?" It's interesting that in verse 23 he's talking about being renewed in the spirit of our mind, but in verse 29 he's talking about our mouth. God knows exactly how we operate. We receive information and then spew it out of our mouth.

You could be walking around, looking real fine, and everyone saying, "Boy, that's a fine young man, that's a lovely young lady." But that's not the proof of the pudding. It's in the talking. That's how we find out what's inside of us because what's on the inside comes out, and sooner or later you'll find out, she looks nice, but she talks awful.

"Let no corrupt communication proceed out of your mouth, but that which is good, to the use of edifying." Do you know there are some things that are in your mind that should never come out of your mouth? Sure, there are some things you hear just in passing. Let them stay right there in our mind; don't let them come out of your mouth.

Start doing a little exercise before you start talking. Stop for a minute and ask some questions before you talk. Put your brain in gear before you let your mouth fly open. Ask yourself, Is this edifying? Is this something I just want to say and was waiting for an opportunity to say it? There's a difference.

Sometimes you have things in your mind and you're just waiting for the opportunity to say it even though you know it's not edifying. We need to follow the example set forth in verse 29, *"Do not let any unwholesome talk come out of your mouths, but only what is helpful for building others up according to their needs, that it may benefit those who listen."*

Verse 30 shows us how a renewed mind operates: "*And do not grieve the Holy Spirit of God, with whom you were sealed unto the day of redemption.*" How do we grieve the Holy Spirit? By allowing our minds to become full of thoughts that are not in line with the Word of God to the point where when the Holy Spirit speaks to us, we do not heed Him at all. One of the jobs of the Holy Spirit is to lead us into all truth.

Jesus, before His crucifixion, said, "*Don't get upset, I'm sending you a Comforter, a Paraclete, One called along side to help.*" The job of the Holy Spirit is to help you in the process of God. The Holy Spirit is there beside you saying, "Yes, do this, this is in line with the Word."

We can grieve the Holy Spirit the same way a child can grieve their parents. The parents are trying their best, sacrificing and so on. The teen goes totally out of bounds of all they've been taught and gets in trouble. They grieve their parents.

Here is the Holy Spirit inside of us telling us everyday, "Go this way. Stay away from those friends, stay with these friends. No, don't hang out there. No, don't put yourself in that position." That's the Holy Spirit on the job. Imagine Him guiding us all day, talking to us. He's telling us to go this way and we keep heading the other way. He's grieved.

We can get to a point where we're no longer even listening to the Holy Spirit because our mind has not been renewed. The Holy Spirit is doing His job, but we are going in another direction. The Holy Spirit hasn't gone anywhere, but you can't hear Him because your mind is so full of junk. You can't distinguish His voice because your mind is so full of your own desires.

Verse 31 tells us, "Get rid of all bitterness, rage and anger, brawling and slander, along with every form of malice." My goodness, look at all the stuff God wants us—in the renewing of our mind—to let go of! Can't we hold onto just a little piece of anger or slander? Isn't that how we feel sometimes? Sometimes we hold onto things because we feel they're going to do us some good. You say, "Well, I can hold onto a little bit of this bitterness." You think it's going to do you some good when all the time it's working against you.

We need to be kind one to another, especially when we're dealing with a brother or sister in the Lord. We're dealing with family, we're members one to another. If you pull down one part of the body, all of the body suffers. Isn't it amazing what God had in mind when He was putting together the body of Christ? We should be kind to our brother or sister because in essence what we're doing is being kind to ourselves.

Verse 32 says, "*Be kind and compassionate to one another, forgiving each other, just as in Christ God forgave you.*" Obviously God knew there would be times when we would need to forgive each other. Yet we're still so surprised when others do things and we have to forgive them. Why is it so difficult to forgive?

When God tells us in His Word, "*Forgive one another,*" notice He makes no distinction about the forgiveness. He doesn't say forgive them if it's unintentional, but if it's intentional let them have it. No, He wants us to forgive whether or not it was intentional.

If we are going to fulfill our responsibility in the process, we need to realize that we have to renew our minds. That's the only way we're going to be able to forgive others. Otherwise, the old nature will tell us to seek revenge.

That last phrase in verse 32 is the key to it all: "*…just as in Christ God forgave you.*" In other words, if someone does something to you that you think is unforgivable, Paul is saying, "If you don't want to forgive them, for nothing else think about the magnitude of your own forgiveness." When we think about the magnitude of our own forgiveness, it becomes unreasonable for us not to forgive someone.

That's exactly what Jesus did when once again the Pharisees thought they had Him in a position where He couldn't do anything. They had brought a woman to Him, saying, "*We caught her in adultery. The law says to stone her. What are You going to do about it?*" All Jesus did was sit and listen while writing something in the dirt. I believe the Pharisees started to see their own sins on the ground. When they saw the magnitude of their own sins, they realized how unreasonable it was to stay and talk about stoning the woman. It was time to leave.

God takes forgiveness to such a magnitude, telling us that if it seems like it's too difficult to forgive, then think about what He does when He forgives us.

Our responsibility in the process of God is to forgive. Our responsibility in the process of God is to renew our minds, which enables us to do everything Paul writes about in Ephesians 4.

We have our responsibility in the process of God. The responsibility that God had, He did. He did what we could not do. God did what you could not do, what it would be impossible for you to do–to die for yourself and forgive yourself. We could not do that; we could not hope to do that.

After God has done the difficult part, He gives us the opportunity to accept His life. He allows us with that new life, with the power of the Holy Spirit inside of us with the Word to fulfill our responsibilities, to work out our salvation, to begin to renew our minds in the process of God.

PROCESS POINTS

- In order to really love the Lord with all your mind, your mind must be renewed.

- Information determines your behavior.

- The most precious gift God ever gave man is the word of God.

- Wrong information will result in wrong decisions.

- The attitude and spirit in which the truth is told is as important as the truth which being told.

- The unrenewed mind is fertile soil for the lies of the enemy.

- Forgiveness of others is the key to your forgiveness.

- Our responsibility in the process of God is to forgive.

Chapter 5

THE TRANSFORMING
PROCESS OF CONFESSION

"Your confession is the conductor of your actions"

"CONFESSION IS A PART OF THE PROCESS OF TRANSFORMATION"

To this day I can still remember having students with me in grade school whose parents would call them names such as stupid or dumb. Not surprisingly, many of those children grew up to become adults who didn't go very far in life. Is it their fault? I would say yes and no. Yes in the sense that we must all take responsibility for our own destiny, but no in the sense that they were greatly influenced by the words constantly confessed over them.

Psychologists would call it self-fulfilling prophecy. The Bible simply says that we will have what we say. Our words have a direct effect on our destiny.

God has an end that has already been determined. Therefore, He can speak about that end, because He already knows the end result of the Word. That's why God, when He speaks to us it's in terms of the end because He knows that the end exists. He knows it's real, and He knows that the Word has inside of it whatever is necessary to take us to the end of the process. God is trying to get us to fulfill our purpose. God speaks about the end, we know that it exists.

Here is something interesting about how God operates His principle. God gives us substance; we call it faith, before we begin the process. God gives "each man a measure" of faith. Why? Because He knows the purpose, and He knows the process we have to go through to get to the purpose. Before we ever begin, God gives us substance to get us to the end because He knows the end. He supplies the faith before the process ever begins.

> *Joshua 1:1-2 says, "After the death of Moses the servant of the Lord, the Lord said to Joshua son of Nun, Moses' aid. 'Moses my servant is dead. Now then, you and all these people, get ready to cross the Jordan River into the land I am about to give to them–to the Israelites."*

God is telling Joshua that He will give him every place where he sets foot, just as He had promised Moses. We continue with Verse 4: "*Your territory will extend from the desert to Lebanon, and from the great river, the Euphrates—all the Hittite country— to the Great Sea on the west.*" Remember, they had not yet crossed into the land. They haven't even seen the land yet, but listen to how God is already talking about the end.

> *Verse 5 says, "No one will be able to stand up against you all the days of your life..." God is giving Joshua and the Israelites substance. He's giving them the faith that they will need to go through the process. They're not yet in the land and haven't even seen anyone yet. God is talking about the end, He's giving them substance.*

> *"...As I was with Moses, so I will be with you; I will never leave you nor forsake you. Be strong and courageous." Why is God saying this? The Israelites haven't seen anything, there is no need to be strong and courageous, they haven't gone into the land yet. Why in the world is God doing this? He's giving them substance.*

Verse 6 continues, "...because you will lead these people to inherit the land I swore to their forefathers to give them. Be strong and very courageous. Be careful to obey all the law my servant Moses gave you."

If we could understand God when He speaks, we'll find it so much easier to operate in faith. God tells the Israelites to be careful to obey all the laws. Why would He tell them that? Because when they get over to the Promised Land, there will be other gods. They will be tempted to obey and follow false gods.

We need to understand what God does when He speaks to us with His words of faith. Nothing that happens surprises God. We're surprised, but we shouldn't be because God takes away the surprises when He speaks to us in faith.

He continues in Joshua 1:7-8, "...do not turn from it to the right or to the left, that you may be successful wherever you go. Do not let this Book of the Law depart from your mouth; meditate on it day and night, so that you may be careful to do everything written in it. Then you will be prosperous and successful."

I believe God is warning the Israelites that there will be other gods around them. God was taking away all of the surprises, everything that the enemy had cooked up. God was exposing it beforehand.

God knew that as the Israelites crossed over, there would be nothing in that land to give them life, only death. So He said, "Don't let this thing depart." He says the same thing to us today: don't let the Word of God depart from you because outside of His Word is death. Inside God's Word is life, so obeying the Word for us is never an option, it is our life. Our life depends on it.

Why was God talking about being strong and courageous, and not to be terrified? Does it mean there were some terrible sights up ahead? Nothing that happens ever surprises God. There's never a day, event, or point in time when we could say, "God, they surprised You, didn't they?"

The Bible has recorded every good and evil thing imaginable. God knows all the tricks. No matter how they may vary, God has them covered. Man never surprises God. God already knows the heart of man. He said a long time ago, "It's desperately wicked."

THE WORD OF GOD GIVES US A SNEAK PREVIEW EVERY TIME.

Any time a situation or crisis arises that could terrify us, we need to look at it and say, "I heard about you, but I ain't afraid."

We can now get a better appreciation why it was considered evil when the reports from the spies came back to Joshua saying the Israelites couldn't take the land. God had already said, "Don't be terrified" because there were some terrible things in there. The Israelites— and we—could look the situation in the eye and say: "Guess what? I heard about you, but I'm not afraid!"

It seems to me that's what David did with Goliath. The young David simply stated, "I heard about you wanting to test the power of God, but I'm not afraid."

Joshua is warned not to get discouraged. He's warned that there will be situations coming up that will make him want to throw up his hands and call it a day. But God tells Joshua that when those times come, look at them and say, "I heard about you, but I'm not discouraged."

There will be situations that make us think we can't get "the land"–we can't get what God's promised us. In these cases, we need to look at the situation and say, "I heard about you and I'm still walking the land." Remember that, as you go through the process of God and come against a situation that was sent to discourage you.

Let's take a look at the word "strategy." Strategy is an intentional word. When a person devises a strategy, it's intentional. In a court of law when there is a crime committed, especially a murder, one of the things the court determines is if it was premeditated. Did the accused plan to do this? Likewise, we need to understand that the enemy has strategies.

When a situation comes to discourage us, that is not a haphazard thing. The enemy planned for that to happen. When this happens, we need to look at that situation and let out a big laugh, saying, "I read about you, but I'm not discouraged because I was told some other things!"

God told Joshua—and tells us—"Don't be terrified, be of good courage, don't be afraid, don't be discouraged." Why? "For the Lord your God will be with you wherever you go." Hallelujah. Throughout a discouraging or terrifying situation, God is with us.

We need to speak to the situation, saying, "I read about you, but I'm not discouraged because the Lord my God is with me." That's what David did. David said, "The same God who was with me when I slew the lion and the bear, will give me your head." In the middle of the ugliest "giant" we may face, God is with us!

As you read through the rest of Joshua's story, you realize that's all he had to hold on to. When Joshua got to Jericho he saw those formidable walls. There may be "walls" you're facing today that are designed to discourage you. The fellow who built those walls didn't build them to encourage you, they're designed to discourage, intimidate and scare you.

When Joshua looked at them, in the natural, I'm sure he said, "Lord, have mercy." He probably went back to God and said, "God, let's talk a minute. Let me make sure I heard You right. You said that You were giving me this land. You did say You were with me wherever, right?"

All Joshua had to hold onto was the Word of God. There weren't any modern inventions for him to say, "Well, OK, we could blow that wall down. We could spring over it. We could fly..." Joshua had none of that stuff. All he had was God's Word.

God started out before they ever crossed the Jordan River by giving them substance. He didn't wait till they got to the walls of Jericho. By the time they hit the walls of Jericho, they had had substance for a long time.

Listen, when we hit walls, we need to understand that we already have substance, our faith. When we hit a wall, we need to realize that we already have faith. Our thinking has always been, "Well, when I hit a wall, I'll go get some faith." No, that's wrong thinking. The Lord has already given you the faith. If Joshua and the Israelites had waited until they hit the walls of Jericho to look for faith, my friend, they would have never made it. They had to be able to rely on a Word from God that they had gotten long before.

Joshua 1:10-11 tells us, "So Joshua ordered the officers of the people: 'Go through the camp and tell the people, 'Get your supplies ready. Three days from now you will cross the Jordan here to go in and take possession of the land."

Look what's happened. Joshua is now doing the talking. When a man starts to speak the Word of God on earth what happens? It starts to become established. Joshua moved from the point of hearing and receiving the Word of God to speaking it. He's now starting to echo what's been in his heart. The thing has now gotten down inside him and it's coming out.

Now, the first time Joshua said this aloud, he might not have really believed it. Some may not agree with me, but I believe Joshua acted out of obedience the first time he spoke these orders. See why obedience is so important? God knows why we need to obey, even when we don't quite believe it.

After Joshua said it the first time he probably stepped back and thought Did I really say that? But it was too late because the people had already started packing. So he said it again, "Get your stuff together, in three days time we're going to possess the land." After he had said it a few times, it had struck a chord deep inside him and he was declaring it with authority, "We're going to possess the land!" At that point, the Israelites started getting it and declaring it to each other, "We're going to possess the land!"

Verses 12-15 say, "But to the Reubenites, the Gadites, and the half tribe of Manasseh, Joshua said, 'Remember the command that Moses the servant of the Lord gave you: 'The Lord your God is giving you rest and has granted you this land.' Your wives, your children and your livestock may stay in the land that Moses gave you east of the Jordan, but all your fighting men, fully armed, must cross over ahead of your brothers. You are to help your brothers until the Lord gives them rest, as he has done for you, and until they too have taken possession of the land that the Lord your God is giving them. After that, you may go back and occupy your own land, which Moses the servant of the Lord gave you east of the Jordan toward the sunrise."

Listen to the reply of the people in Verse 16: "*Then they answered Joshua, 'Whatever you have commanded us we will do.'*" What a powerful response! What would have happened if Joshua had not believed God? The Israelites at this point might have had a totally different reaction.

Instead the people are behind Joshua one hundred percent. They're saying, "Just as we saw God work with Moses." The people are starting to build their faith. Somewhere along the way, the people stopped and thought and said, "You know, God was with Moses and we saw God do some miraculous things that we really couldn't understand. When we left Egypt we didn't know what would happen, but we saw God come through. Something is going on."

Their faith, the evidence, the substance from the beginning started to now rise up inside the people. They said to Joshua, "Based on what we have seen God do before with Moses, if God will be with you like He was with Moses, that's all we ask."

They transferred their obedience from Joshua to God. By the time they had finished, they had put their obedience in God. Their approach was, "It doesn't make much sense to us to march around a wall, but if you say march because God told you, we'll march."

Sometimes, in the middle of our situations, we need to stop for a minute and say, "God, I don't understand why You're telling me to just stand now because I don't see anything happening. I don't understand it, but you said to stand so I'll stand. Based on your reputation, based on your past performance, I will do what You asked me to do."

God's reputation, His past actions is substance—or faith. When the people replied, "All we ask Joshua, is that God be with you as He was with Moses," my friend, they were serious about that. So serious that in verse 18 they say, "Whoever rebels against your word and does not obey your words, whatever you may command them, will be put to death." That's how serious they were in their believing.

God speaks about the end because He wants to give you substance to go through the process. He spoke to Joshua as if they were already in the land. As far as God was concerned, the land was already theirs.

God has destined us for success. Think about that for one second. We don't really understand, we really don't, how much God has destined us for success. Could I use another word? God has programmed each of us for success. Just as a seed has been programmed to produce a certain fruit, plant, crop or flower, we are programmed to succeed.

Our adversary tries to tell us otherwise, but do you realize that a seed is not supposed to have to struggle to bring forth fruit? It's just supposed to do it. I use the word programmed because we're such a computer society now. What you put into a computer, is what comes out. Whatever you program into the computer that will come out. You don't have to say, "Well, I wonder if this thing will come out?"

In the same way, we shouldn't struggle to succeed because we were already programmed to succeed. The adversary tries to convince us that we're not supposed to succeed, but ever since the beginning of time, according to what I read, everything was created what? Good. Not "kind of good" or "almost good" or "not good if there is struggle," but good. The original intent and program was success. Success was written all over Adam and Eve.

God already decided that man is supposed to be a success. We don't have to wonder about that, God already decided it. Just as He's already decided that the seed should bring forth fruit or flower.

In Genesis 12:1:2 God tells Abraham: "Leave your country, your people and your father's household and go to the land I will show you. I will make you into a great nation."

You have to understand the scene. Abraham was an old man when God first appeared to him. He had no idea what God was talking about yet God gives him substance. God didn't say, "Maybe I can make you a great nation." No, there was no doubt in God's Word. He was giving Abraham pure substance: "*I will make you into a great nation, I will bless you, I will make your name great, and you will be a blessing. I will bless those who bless you*" (Gen. 12:2-3). See what I mean about the children of God being programmed for success? It sounds like success to me–not failure.

"And whoever curses you I will curse; and all peoples on earth will be blessed through you. So Abram left, as the Lord had told him; and Lot went with him. Abram was seventy-five years old when he set out from Haran. He took his wife Sarai, his nephew Lot, all the possessions they'd accumulated, and the people they had acquired in Haran, and they set out for the land of Canaan and they arrived there" (Gen. 12:3-5).

What I want you to see is this: Abraham believed to the point of taking all of his possessions. Do we have enough faith to believe to the point of obeying all the way? You know, he could have said, "Well, I don't know too much about this land you talking about, but I kind of believe you. Tell you what I'll do, I'll go ahead and do a little scouting. If it looks right, I'll come back for my family and possessions." Or, he could've said, "I'll take some of my possessions because I just don't know about this land. If things look right, I'll come back for the rest. But if things don't look right, I'm going back where the rest is."

Instead, Abraham had enough faith from His encounter with God to believe Him to the point that he would take all of his family and all of his possessions. Do we have enough faith to believe all the way like that? You see why Abram was called the father of the faithful?

God speaks about the end because it exists, it's real. He speaks about the end to give us some substance. He speaks about the end to give us something to say in the middle.

I believe by the time Joshua and the Israelites hit Jericho, they had remembered the beginning and said, "You know, God said something in the beginning. Let's march! He said He would be with us wherever we went. He told us not to be afraid. Let's go, let's march!" They had something to say in the middle, so He spoke it from the beginning because He had already seen the end. The end existed.

Whatever God says, it exists, it's real. When He tells you to "be courageous," the courage is there, it exists, and it's real. You're not just talking out your head it exists, why? God said it exists. If God said it, it's real, it's real.

When God told Moses to deliver the children of Israel, He said He would be with them. Their deliverance would be real, but they couldn't see it. They had no way of knowing how they would get through the wilderness. When they came to the Red Sea, Moses couldn't figure out a solution. But their deliverance existed in the most unlikely place–right through the middle of the water.

Right in the middle of our process our deliverance is there, in the most unlikely places. We would have thought it would be around the water–but God's not bothered by water! Whatever your situation is, God is not bothered by it. God is not surprised and He's not bothered. There is no situation that can catch God off guard. There's never a time when the enemy can say, "Well, I got You now. I'll throw this one on You. I know You weren't ready for this."

God is ready all the time. He's already seen the end. That's what the devil didn't realize with Jesus. Jesus had already seen the end and there's the devil in the middle saying, "I got Him, I got Him, I got Him." But God knew–He could see an empty tomb and this silly devil talking about how he got Jesus.

God has destined us for success, but we need to remember to say something. Start saying, "I recognize you situation, but I was told something else about you. My God is with me.

PROCESS POINTS

- God gives us substance called faith.

- God always gives a sneak preview of purpose..

- God operates based on his reputation.

- God speaks about the end because He wants to give you substance to complete the process.

- God has programmed us for success.

- Whatever God says exists, it is real.

- Deliverance is in the middle of the process.

- Our confession is our agreement with God.

God has destined us for success and waits for our agreement.

Chapter 6

THE LIFE PRINCIPLE
OF PROCESS

"Life is the gift of God, but is capital that must be spent or it dissipates"

-- Charles Templeton

"THE PRINCIPLE OF PROCESS IS A LIFE-LING ONE AND ENABLES US TO GO FROM PURPOSE TO PURPOSE."

It is interesting to note that every person on earth is desirous of receiving, even if in some instances it is done illegally and without "due process." Everyone wants the blessing of God, but not everyone is prepared for the process of God. However, there can never be the blessing of God without the process of God. That's simply the way God has designed the system. In fact, life itself operates on the principle of process before reward, giving before receiving, investment before return, and work before compensation.

Let's take a look at some aspects of David's life. I'll call this a look at "A Citizen in the Process," which is all of us. We all fit in that category because we're all citizens in the process of God. None of us have arrived yet, but we are on our way.

In fact, the process of God is a lifetime process. You don't arrive until you leave the earth. In 1 Samuel 16:1-3 we see the Lord choosing David: *"The Lord said to Samuel, 'How long will you mourn for Saul? Since I have rejected him as king over Israel; fill your horn with oil and be on your way. I'm sending you to Jesse of Bethlehem; I have chosen one of his sons to be king.'*

"But Samuel said, 'How can I go, Saul will hear about it and kill me?' The Lord said, 'Take a heifer with you and say, 'I have come to sacrifice to the Lord.' Invite Jesse to the sacrifice, and I will show you what to do. You are to anoint for Me the one I indicate.'"

Let's skip down to verses 6-13: "When they arrived, Samuel saw Eliab, and thought, 'Surely the Lord's anointed stands here before the Lord.' But the Lord said to Samuel, 'Do not consider his appearance or his height, for I have rejected him. The Lord does not look at the things man looks at, man looks at the outward appearance, but the Lord looks at the heart.'"

"Then Jesse called Abinadab and had him pass in front of Samuel. But Samuel said, 'The Lord has not chosen this one either.' Jesse then had Shammah pass by, but Samuel said, 'Nor has the Lord chosen this one.' Jesse had seven of his sons pass before Samuel, but Samuel said to him, 'The Lord has not chosen these.' So he asked Jesse, 'Are these all the sons you have?' 'There is still the youngest,' Jesse answered, 'but he is tending the sheep.' Samuel said, 'Send for him; we will not sit down until he arrives.'

"So he sent and had him brought in. He was ruddy, with a fine appearance and handsome features. Then the Lord said, 'Rise and anoint him; he is the one.' So Samuel took the horn of oil and anointed him in the presence of his brothers, and from that day on the Spirit of the Lord came upon David in power. Samuel then went to Ramah."

There are some interesting things in this passage about the process of God and how God chooses us. David was actually what you might call the least likely candidate to be anointed king. Has anyone ever told you that you're an unlikely candidate for success or greatness?

First of all, David was the youngest, which means you would consider him to be very inexperienced. As far as appearances, some of his older brothers probably looked more like kingship material. Perhaps they looked statelier, had more stature.

Isn't it interesting that in the process of God, He looks for potential? God has a way of looking at us and choosing us because of what He sees on the inside. There are qualities God sees in us that are not visible yet. God does not look at outward appearances, He looks at the heart. He sees the potential we have inside us, of fulfilling what He is calling us to do.

Where you're at doesn't determine whether or not God wants to use you. That's where we miss it many times in the process of God. We look at where we're at when God says He wants us to do something with our lives. We say, "But God, this is where I'm at. I can't possibly do that."

God is saying, "Friend, I'm not looking at where you are at. I'm looking at where I'm going to take you. I'm looking at your heart and your willingness to obey Me." That's all God is looking at.

God is not necessarily looking at our "professionalism." If they had been choosing candidates for a king by giving an exam, David probably would've flunk. He was not professional enough. But God is not looking at whether or not we're "experts." When God chooses us, He looks at our willingness to be used by Him. That's the major criteria He uses.

God is not limited by our ability; He is limited only by our willingness to be used. God is not limited by where you're at in your ability at this point, that doesn't limit God. He is bigger than that. After all, He's the creator. He can give you whatever He wants to give you.

A spiritual call and responsibility have nothing to do with appearance; it has nothing to do with age. God chooses men and women who have potential to go through the process.

Being chosen to go through the process of God does not mean you will go through it. It simply means you have the potential to go through it. Being chosen does not mean you are exempt from fleshly failures. Being chosen does not mean you are perfect, otherwise no one would be chosen. Being chosen does not mean God will not punish your sin. We'll see that proven as we look at David's life.

Here was David, a young shepherd being chosen and anointed to be king, knowing nothing about what it meant to be king. All this young man knew was how to take care of his father's sheep. Many of us feel like David at times when the Lord begins to give us a glimpse of our purpose.

Do you realize what the Lord has said to us as citizens? He can do above what we can think or imagine. We can think and imagine some tremendous things, but God is saying, "I've got news for you. I can do above that." The best that you can think, God says, "I can do above that."

How can He make a statement like that? Because He knows that if you are willing to go through the process, He will do it. There's no limitation with God.

God saw some potential in David that had not yet surfaced. In 1 Samuel 17:32-34 David goes to see his brothers and upon arriving at the battlefront, sees a distressing scene.

"David said to Saul, 'Let no one lose heart on account of this Philistine, your servant will go and fight him.' Saul replied, *'You are not able to go out against this Philistine and fight him; you are only a boy, and he has been a fighting man from his youth.'* As far as the king was concerned, David was disqualified due to his age and lack of experience.

"But David said to Saul, 'Your servant has been keeping his father's sheep.'" It really doesn't matter what you have been doing in the process. It really doesn't matter where God has placed you in the body, in the process. What matters is what you have learned while in the process. You have to appreciate the fact that in Saul's army, there were soldiers who had been soldiers from their youth. They had not learned the things that David had learned tending his father's sheep.

God knows what He wants to do with us. He knows where we're at and if we will learn what He wants to teach us. We will find out as we go along in the process that we will come to a place and point in time where we will be able to say, "You know, I was obeying God in this area and He taught me some principles."

David continues in Verses 34-36: "Your servant has been keeping his father's sheep. When a lion and a bear came and carried off a sheep from the flock, I went after it, struck it and rescued the sheep from its mouth. When it turned on me, I seized it by its hair, struck it and killed it. Your servant has killed both the lion and the bear; this uncircumcised Philistine will be like one of them, because he has defied the armies of the living God."

As far as David was concerned, he had learned that opposition was opposition. He didn't have to wait until he was king to understand opposition. It didn't matter whether it was a lion, a bear or a giant. He had learned how to deal with opposition in the process.

In Verse 37 he says,

"The Lord who delivered me from the paw of the lion and the paw of the bear will deliver me from the hand of this Philistine.' Saul said to David, 'Go, and the Lord be with you.'"

Verses 40-47 say,

"Then he took his staff in his hand, chose five smooth stones from the stream, put them in the pouch of his shepherd's bag and, with his sling in his hand, approached the Philistine. Meanwhile, the Philistine, with his shield bearer in front of him, kept coming closer to David. He looked David over and saw that he was only a boy, ruddy and handsome, and he despised him. He said to David, 'Am I a dog, that you come at me with sticks?' And the Philistine cursed David by his gods. 'Come here,'

*he said, 'and I'll give your flesh to the birds of the air and the beasts of
the field!'*

*"David said to the Philistine, 'You come against me with sword and
spear and javelin, but I come against you in the name of the Lord
Almighty, the God of the armies of Israel, whom you have defiled. This
day the Lord will hand you over to me, and I'll strike you down and cut
off your head. Today I will give the carcasses of the Philistine army to
the birds of the air and the beasts of the earth, and the whole world will
know that there is a God in Israel. All those gathered here will know
that it is not by sword or spear that the Lord saves; for the battle is the
Lord's, and he will give all of you into our hands.'"*

In the process God is continually teaching us principles to pre-
pare us for the next step. It is evident that David the shepherd boy
had learned courage. Have you learned courage where you're at?
Courage rises to the forefront. Why? Because in the process God
wants you to understand that when obstacles come, that's when
courage is to rise up. Not fear, but courage. David had learned
courage and it rose up. God wants to develop in us courage in
the process.

We also see very readily that David had confidence. Look at his
statement in verse 34 to Saul, "'your servant has been keeping his
father's sheep.'" David uses his experience to build up his confidence. He had confidence in God's ability because of what he had
already experienced.

God takes you through the process to build in you a confidence
that you will need as you go along. What if David hadn't learned
confidence and courage while taking care of the sheep? He had
been called, chosen and anointed to be king, but it seemed he was
totally unqualified. Yet, at the point where the nation was about
to be wiped out, who comes on the scene?

*Verse 37 says, "The Lord who delivered me from the paw of the lion
and the paw of the bear will deliver me from the hand of this Philistine."*

We must have a relationship with God in order to receive from
Him, in order to know Him. Even as a young shepherd boy

David obviously had such a relationship with God that he had a revelation of His might and power.

Sometimes when you run from opportunities, you miss your lesson, you miss the chance to understand how big God really is. That's why He tells us to welcome trials. Why? Because we'll understand how big God is in the midst of that situation. If David had run when the bear came, he would have missed his lesson in the process. Obviously he embraced the opportunity and learned a great lesson from it.

What have you done with your last lesson? Did you embrace the opportunity to experience the bigness of God or did you try to bypass the exercise?

In Verses 46-47 David boldly declares to Goliath: "This day the Lord will hand you over to me." Did David simply walk out there and say, "Oh, there's a giant. No problem, I'll get him." No, he said, "This day the Lord will hand him over." David had learned that he needed to be willing to always give the glory and credit to God. Why? Because it was the Lord who did it. If David had walked out and said, "Well, God helped me with the lion and the bear, but I can handle this one by myself," it would have been a totally different story.

David was always willing to give the credit to God. Who do you give the credit to with your successes and victories? Do you say, "I did it on my own strength, my own intelligence"? If it was God, you need to give glory and credit to Him. David was willing not to hold onto the credit, but to give the credit to God.

In addition, David was not afraid of shadows. He was not afraid of voices, even the voice of a booming giant. Verse 41 tells us: "Meanwhile the Philistine, with his shield bearer in front of him, kept coming closer to David. He looked David over." By now David had seen how big this giant really was, and Goliath sees that David is just a boy.

The story continues in Verses 41-44:

> "...and he (Goliath) despised him. He said to David 'Am I a dog that you come at me with sticks?' And the Philistine cursed David by his

gods. 'Come here,' he said, 'and I'll give your flesh to the birds of the air and the beasts of the field!"

What do you do when you hear voices? Some of us run so fast, simply because we heard something or saw a shadow. Sometimes the devil doesn't even have to touch us. With some of us all he has to do is speak and we take off running.

He plays a head game with us. That's how fighters operate; they get ugly and say what they're going to do. They try to psych out their opponent, hoping they won't show. Or, if they do show, they'll be so scared that they won't be able to do anything.

As God takes you through the process, you have to understand that the shadows and the voices can't do anything to you. They're only meant to scare you off. Why would someone try to scare you off? I believe the answer is simple: they're frightened of you.

If the enemy is trying to frighten you away from what God said you could do, it's because he believes you could do it. He understands that the God inside of you can do exactly what He told you He can do. Take heart–the enemy can only frighten you!

Obviously David already had learned out in the field that even if the lion growled, it didn't make his power any greater. Remember, "Greater is He that is in you than he that is in the world." It really doesn't matter what the one in the world does.

In 2 Samuel 2, David is anointed king over Judah. In chapter 5 he's anointed king over Israel. In chapter 8 he goes on, because of the process of God, to win tremendous victories.

Second Samuel 8:1-4 tells us,

"In the course of time David defeated the Philistines and subdued them, and he took Methe-gammah from the control of the Philistines. David also defeated the Moabites, He made them lie down on the ground, and measured them off with length of cord, every two lengths of them were put to death. And the third length was allowed to live. So the Moabites became subject to David, and brought tribute.

"Moreover David fought Hadadezer, the son of Rehob, king of Zobah, when he went to restore his control along the Euphrates River. David captured a thousand of his chariots, seven thousand charioteers, and twenty thousand foot soldiers. He hamstrung all but a hundred of the chariot horses."

As I said before, it doesn't pay to try to cut the process short. If you short-cut the process, you're not going to be able to fulfill God's purpose for your life. God's blessing is in the midst of the process; it's in the midst of the lessons He's trying to teach you.

As time goes on, we see David, this great king who had a tremendous heart for God, fall into temptation. Isn't it interesting that the Bible does not hide it at all? That's what I appreciate about God's Word, it doesn't hide faults and mistakes. We know that even though David was a citizen of the kingdom, even though he was going through the process, and had done tremendous things, he missed something along the way.

We pick up the story in 2 Samuel 11:1: *"In the spring, at the time when kings go off to war,"* David was king so what was he doing home? He should have been off at war. This was David's first problem, he was out of position.

"David sent Joab out with the king's men and the whole Israelite army. They destroyed the Ammonites and besieged Rabbah, but David remained in Jerusalem." You've got to be in the right position, don't be out of place. Perhaps sometimes we are in the wrong place. God tells us to do something, go somewhere, and we decide to do something else. We allow ourselves to be caught by the enemy through our own doing, our own disobedience.

One night David got up from his bed and walked around on the roof of the palace. From his vantage point he saw a very beautiful woman bathing. Since he was the king, he figured he could do what he wanted. So he sent for the woman, and you know the rest of that story. The woman went back home, and then, according to 2 Samuel: *"The woman conceived and sent word to David saying, 'I'm pregnant'"* (2 Sam. 11:5).

David was going through the process, but he missed something. "So David sent this word to Joab, Send me Uriah the Hittite. And Joab sent him to David" (2 Sam. 11:6), and we know how David tried his best. Obviously Uriah the Hittite was a man of principles and character, and he refused to go home. How could he go home, he said, while his men were out fighting?

David was a man chosen by God for a specific purpose. God would not allow him to simply walk away from that, so God did something very interesting.

In 2 Samuel 12:1-13, it says God sent Nathan to David. Nathan tells him the story about the two men, one rich, one poor, and David listened. Verse 5 says, *"David burned with anger against the man and said to Nathan, 'As surely as the Lord lives, the man who did this deserves to die! He must pay for that lamb four times over, because he did such a thing and had no pity.'*

> *"Then Nathan said to David, 'You are the man! This is what the Lord, the God of Israel, says, 'I anointed you king over Israel, and I delivered you from the hand of Saul. I gave your master's house to you, and your master's wives into your arms. I gave you the house of Israel and Judah. And if all this had been too little, I would have given you even more. Why did you despise the word of the Lord by doing what is evil in his eyes? You struck down Uriah the Hittite with the sword and took his wife to be your own. You killed him with the sword of the Ammonites. Now, therefore, the sword will never depart from your house, because you despised me and took the wife of Uriah the Hittite to be your own.'*

> *"This is what the Lord says, 'Out of your own household I am going to bring calamity upon you. Before your very eyes I will take your wives and give them to one who is close to you, and he will lie with your wives in broad daylight. You did it in secret, but I will do this thing in broad daylight before all Israel.'"*

"THEN DAVID SAID TO NATHAN, 'I HAVE SINNED AGAINST THE LORD.'"

I want you to see some things here about the process of God when we sin. The first thing is that, even though God chooses us,

He leaves our will intact. He still gives us the option of obeying Him or disobeying Him. He still gives us the right to sin if we want to sin. David learned; his will was intact. It would have been nice if the Lord had said, "Give Me your will so you don't make any stupid mistakes," but He didn't.

Secondly, we must protect our mind and control our body in the midst of the process of God. God expects us to do so. In the process of God, God's responsibility to us is to do what He has promised through us as we submit ourselves to Him. And then He gives us the ability to control our mind and bodies. He gives us the right to choose to draw on His ability to help us.

Thirdly, citizens in the process are still capable of almost anything. I want you to think about that for a minute. We have to be careful when we start to judge. By any standards that you want to use, you would have to agree with me that David obviously was a great man of God. But how did this chosen mighty king of Israel do something like this? Easy, he was still in the process. He was still learning. He had not arrived at immortality simply because he was anointed king.

In the process of God, as I have stated earlier, you have not arrived until you leave the earth. David was still in the process of God. Men and women of God commit sins and do things, and people wonder, How could they do that? They're still in the process. Paul says, if I may paraphrase, "While I'm correcting, I'm very careful because I'm still in the process."

Many citizens of the kingdom fall because they mistakenly think they've arrived at the end of the process. However, that's right when the enemy says, "Great! Now I can slip this one in because their guard is down."

For the rest of our lives, we are all in the process. If we ever let our guard down, that's when the enemy takes advantage of us. It doesn't matter who you are or what position you have in the body of Christ, all of us are in the process of God. It's a continually ongoing process.

What I like about David is that he knew what to do when he had sinned in the process. That's what we need to learn. What do you do when you sin in the process? In 2 Samuel 12 it says that Nathan came and rebuked David. In the process of God, He requires holiness.

I love what David said in verse 13: *"I have sinned against the Lord."* David didn't say he sinned against Uriah the Hittite, he said, "I've sinned against God." David understood that when we as citizens of the kingdom of God sin, we sin against God. God is the One who establishes righteousness. Even when people commit crimes, they're really sinning against God because the laws that we have in our nations are really patented and based on the Word of God. Not everybody will admit it, but that's really where we got the idea of right and wrong.

What should we do when we sin in the process? First, we need to agree with God that it is sin. That sounds so simple, but that's where we miss it sometimes. We want to instead rationalize it and give excuses. We have to call it what it is–sin.

Secondly, we need to make a decision to stop. That also sounds simple, but it's the simple things that hang us up. Make a decision to stop. Sometimes people know they have missed in the process, and instead of stopping they continue.

Third, repent of it and turn the other way. Sin does not terminate the process; it merely hinders growth by stopping the flow of life. Life for us comes from God. Sin hinders that flow of life. When we sin, as citizens in the process, the process is not over. God is not finished with us. He doesn't give up on us, but our sin blocks the flow of His life to us.

Unrepentance—or, an unwillingness to repent—can terminate the process of God in your life. Nothing else can stop the process because God has made provisions if we fall.

When we sin, we need to realize that God is not finished with us. We may have blockage, but it's not over. We take the same three steps that David took and we keep moving.

Psalms 51 records David's cry after he sinned: "*Have mercy on me, O God, according to your unfailing love; according to your great compassion blot out my transgressions. Wash away all my iniquity and cleanse me from my sin.*"

That sounds like a man who has faced the facts and agreed with God that he sinned.

He continues, "I know my transgressions, and my sin is always before me. Against you, you only, have I sinned and done what is evil in your sight, so that you are proved right when you speak, and justified when you judge. Surely I was sinful at birth, sinful from the time my mother conceived me. Surely you desire truth in the inner parts; you teach me wisdom in the inmost place. Cleanse me with hyssop, and I will be clean; wash me, and I will be whiter than snow. Let me hear joy and gladness; Let the bones you have crushed rejoice. Hide your face from my sins and blot out all my iniquity. Create in me a pure heart, O God, and renew a steadfast spirit within me."

There's David's cry for God again. In other words, "God, let's get back in the process, give me a clean heart again. I don't want to stop what You've started."

"Do not cast me from your presence or take your Holy Spirit from me. Restore to me the joy of your salvation, and grant me a willing spirit to sustain me. Then I will teach transgressors your ways, and sinners will turn back to you."

What a heart, what a cry to God for mercy! David understood that in the process of God, sin is not termination of the process. Psalm 51 is a great psalm to remember, but you've got to mean it when you say it.

"Save me from blood guilt, O God, the God who saves me, and my tongue will sing of your righteousness. O Lord, open my lips, and my mouth will declare your praise. You do not delight in sacrifice, or I would bring it; you do not take pleasure in burnt offerings. The sacrifices of God are of a broken spirit; a broken and contrite heart, O God, you will not despise.

"In your good pleasure make Zion prosper; build up the walls of Jerusalem. Then there will be righteous sacrifices, whole burnt offerings to delight you; then bulls will be offered on your altar."

The end product of the process of God is the character of God.

PROCESS POINTS

- Life itself operates on the principle of process before reward.

- In the process of God, God looks for potential.

- God is not limited by our ability as much as He is limited by our willing to be used.

- Present principles are the preparation for the next step in the process.

- Circumstances will either force you to experience the bigness of God or you will shun the opportunity.

- The adversary will only seek to frighten those he is frightened of.

- God's blessing is in the midst of the lessons He is trying to teach you.

- God chooses, but he never negates our will.

- Unrepentance can terminate the process of God in your life.

The end product of the process of God is the character of God.

Chapter 7

BLESSINGS ARE IN THE PROCESS

"Adopt the pace of nature; her secret is patience"

--Ralph Waldo Emerson

"He that can have patience can have what he will"

--Benjamin Franklin

"THE PROCESS OF PURPOSE MAY SEEM FRUIT-LESS, BUT THE BLESSING IS IN THE PROCESS"

We can learn an important principle from the growth process of a seed. It begins its growth process in the ground–so the plant is growing and we can't even see it. Sometimes we get impatient for the fruit and eat fruit that is not ripe, not mature. If you've ever done this you know the benefit of patiently waiting for the fruit to grow into full maturity.

In Matthew 13 Jesus explains the parable of the sower to His disciples. It's a story that effectively illustrates the effects of the truth of God's Word in our lives. We see that the Word goes forth and falls on different types of soil. When it falls on rocky soil, it's very likely that we won't see much fruit come forth in that person's life. Likewise, if it falls on a path and birds come along and eat it, we won't see much produced in that person's life either.

Often God's Word falls inside the church and you get the Word because you're sitting in the church, but what do you do with the Word? More than likely that's determined by what happens when you leave the church and walk back out into the world. I believe that's where the enemy is waiting to steal the Word from you. He was bound up inside the church, but he's waiting outside the church doors to steal the Word from you. He wants to get it out of you before you have an opportunity to do anything with it.

Maybe you've wondered why so-and-so is a Christian. They go to church every Sunday and hear the Word of God preached in a powerful way, but you don't see any change in their life or attitude. It's very likely that as they walk out those church doors every Sunday, the devil jumps them and says, "Give me this Word." It's taken out of their heart before they even had an opportunity to do anything with it.

In Matthew 13:11 Jesus says something in this parable that's very important: *"He replied, 'The knowledge of the secrets of the kingdom of heaven has been given to you, but not to them.'"*

God has kept nothing back on how we are to operate as citizens in the kingdom of God, as new creatures in Christ. He's kept nothing back from us. He has given us everything we need to know in how to do that which we're supposed to do, and to know how to be exactly what we're supposed to be.

When someone tells you a secret, it's usually a very important piece of information and they hold onto it before sharing it with you. When they think the time is right they say, "Have I got a secret for you." God has a secret—on how we can operate in the kingdom. But He has given it freely and openly to us. He's not kept back anything. We have no excuses, no reasons for not becoming everything God wants us to be. If we want the principles of the kingdom to work for us, we must understand that the manifestation of the Word of God is the key to how they're going to work.

Let's read on in Matthew 13:12:

> *"Whoever has will be given more, and he will have an abundance. Whoever does not have, even what he has will be taken from him."*

At first it may sound like God is not being fair; that He would give more to those who already have abundance and take away from those who don't even have anything. But in actuality, what He's saying is this–when the Word of God falls on your heart and your heart is good soil, you're open to receiving it.

If God's Word affects you to the point that it changes your lifestyle, which is really what being a Christian is all about, when you hear more of it, you'll receive more.

On the other hand, if a person hears God's Word—even just a little bit—and loses it because they can't hang onto it, the enemy will take it away. Why? Because it had no affect on the person. They didn't receive it. They merely heard it, but didn't understand it. When we speak of really hearing something, we're talking about really understanding it.

Don't we all want to be the type of believer who receives the Word of God to the point that it truly affects our life? Then, we're open to receiving some more, we're ready for more. Why are we ready for more? Because the Bible says, "Line upon line, precept upon precept."

We get the first line, and man oh man we're reading to see how this next line is going to line up. We're waiting to see how it's going to come together, how this picture is going to come out. We can't wait to find out. So we get the next line and grapple over that thing. It all starts to come together as we read and understand the rest–soon it's precept upon precept. We can't wait to get it because we know when we get this piece, it's going to make more sense. We're going to understand how to do things better. Our life, our attitude, our relationships start to change.

Then there's the person who hears God's Word and lets it go in one ear and out the other. When they hear more, their reaction is, "Oh, that's good. Man that's good." But they don't hold onto it. They never take hold of the Word and put it inside their heart. They're not going to be saying, "Oh, this is some good teaching." Why? Because it's not affecting them. It's not doing anything for them.

God never meant for His Word to simply be admired. That's not what He intended. He was not after us to simply say, "That was a good word, Reverend." That's what the Scribes and Pharisees did. They were jam-packed with the Word of God, but all they were doing with it was holding it up and saying, "This came from Abraham. Boy, its good stuff and we got it and those other fellows don't. Look at them."

Then Jesus came along, read from Isaiah and said, "By the way, this Scripture is fulfilled today." Those fellows didn't know what to do. They knew Scripture backwards and forwards. They could recite it in their sleep, but when Scripture was fulfilled right in front of them they didn't know what it meant. Some of us are the same way. We can repeat some Scripture backwards and forwards, but we don't know what it truly means. It's because God's Word has not affected us yet; it's not done a thing to us.

Did you ever notice in school that the student who sits there and listens to the teacher gets more out of school than the other kids? Everyone thinks, Wow, that's one smart kid. Well, maybe he is, but it's probably due in a large part to the fact that he's listening with a receptive mind. The other kids are sitting there getting nothing because they're too busy talking to friends, playing or daydreaming.

If the manifestation of God's Word is the key to the secret of His kingdom, then why doesn't the Word just work? Why don't things just happen? I've got three reasons why it doesn't work like that:

Number One: Because you live in this world.

Number Two: Because you are in this flesh.

Number Three: Because the devil is a reality and he does not like you.

There will always be opposition to God's Word from one of those three reasons–or all at one time.

Let's look at number one: the world. When I speak of the world I don't mean simply this physical location. I'm talking about a world system, a way of thinking and a way of doing things that has been handed down to us by the god of this world.

When we come to the Lord Jesus our spirits are saved, but much to our dismay our minds are not. Even though we're now Christians, we're still living in a world that's been greatly influenced by the Garden of Eden from way back in the time of Genesis. See how many years this thing has been influenced by the god of this world? Not just ten years or even a thousand, but thousands of years of influence and guess what? You live right in the middle of this world.

The Lord wants to show us how to be in this world, but not of it. He's not going to take us out of this world to show us how to operate in this world. That's what we would like, but that's not going to happen.

God wants to show you that by the very process of living in this world—if you will operate by the principles of that world—you will receive the blessings He promised in His Word.

Paul says in 2 Corinthians 4:1-2,

"Therefore, since through God's mercy we have this ministry, we do not lose heart. Rather, we have renounced secret and shameful ways; we do not use deception, nor do we distort the word of God. On the contrary, by setting forth the truth plainly we commend ourselves to every man's conscience in the sight of God."

Some people ask me, "Why do you think some Christians come to God, but end up returning to their old habits and old ways?"

Well, in looking at what Paul says, some Christians have simply asked forgiveness, but they haven't renounced it. There's a difference. The Lord forgives us when we ask Him to, but we also have to renounce that sin, that old bad habit. We have to reach that point where we believe that sin will kill us if we don't let it go. That sin, that habit is totally against God and we shouldn't want anything to do with it.

When your youngster does something wrong and you respond with love saying, "Now why did you do that?" They give you some excuse and you say, "OK, don't do it anymore." Even if they totally agree with you and seem truly sorry, I can guarantee you, give them a little while and they'll do it again. Why? They didn't renounce that behavior. They were sorry because they knew what was coming.

Some of us are sorry at the time because we know what's coming. So we say, "I'm sorry Lord," but you don't renounce your sinful behavior. People can stop any kind of behavior they want if they're convinced enough that their behavior is against God. If it's sinful and it won't help you–you can stop it.

How many of you will walk up to your gas stove and put your finger in the fire and hold it there? No because that would be painful, destructive and foolish. You're so convinced that if you put your finger in that flame it will burn you and hurt a great deal. Well, if you're that convinced about the fire, why not be that convinced about sinful habits in your life?

It's the same decision-making process. God didn't convince you by the fire. He didn't come with a revelation and tell you, "Thou shalt not touch the fire." You didn't have to get any sign, right?

So why do Christians say things like, "I'm waiting for the Lord to tell me to stop doing such and so." I've got news for them, the Lord did tell them. He told them the minute He forgave them of their sins. How much more telling do they need? What else are they waiting for?

People are not convinced enough to renounce certain things in their life because it's not yet a conviction. Do you see what happens when you're not convinced enough? You leave room for the enemy. The devil doesn't make you do it, but you give him some room, so he jumps in.

Some Christians are not to the point where they will renounce secret and shameful ways. They want someone to pray for them. No one prayed for you to yank your finger out of the fire—you didn't wait on any prayers, right? You tried it once and that was it. Immediately you knew that was no place to put your finger.

Second Corinthians 4:2-4 continues:

"...nor do we distort the word of God. On the contrary, by setting forth the truth plainly we commend ourselves to every man's conscience in the sight of God. And even if our gospel is veiled, it is veiled to those who are perishing. The god of this age has blinded the minds of unbelievers, so that they cannot see the light of the gospel of the glory of Christ, who is the image of God."

The god of this world, or of this age, has blinded what? The minds of unbelievers. Notice that he doesn't blind the spirit. The devil knows that he can try to persuade people to think his thoughts or to do things the way he has set them down in the world's system.

To operate in faith, you've got to understand certain things. In this world's system, the devil is out to constantly blind our minds. That is, to keep us from being able to think according to God's Word and in line with the Word of God–His truth. The enemy tries so hard to keep the truth from us.

Not many Christians believe that we don't have to use our mind, just our spirit. The devil is smarter than us because he knows that we can't appropriate the things of the spirit through our mind. We receive from God through our spirits, yes, but we interpret what we receive through our minds. So our minds have to be in line with the truth of the Word of God. We can interpret what we receive properly. If the devil can cause us, through his system of thinking, to think something other than the truth, we will never be able to really interpret what God is saying. We will never be able to apply what God has given us in His Word because the devil is dealing with our mind.

The god of this world is out to keep people's minds blinded. As Christians we do not worship our minds. Let me make that clear, I'm not advocating that you worship your mind. We have more sense than that. We use our minds and we put in our minds the truth of God's Word so that our minds will work for us and not us working for our minds. There's a difference there. There's a point where you can be working for your mind. You think, I've just got to learn all this! You're working for your mind; your mind is not working for you.

We have to use our minds. We need to renew our minds. That's why the Bible tells us: renew it so you can use it. This is so that we will be able to interpret what God gives us in the spirit through our mind. God desires for us to renew our mind so that we are able to think the right thoughts and interpret correctly what He is telling us.

We don't worship our minds, we use them. We make our minds serve us by learning how to obey God's Word. We can stop and tap into the secret of the kingdom, which is what? The operation of the world. That's how you're going to know the secret of the kingdom–the secret of how to live in the kingdom of God and to be able to properly operate the Word of God in your life.

The god of this age deceives unbelievers into believing that they are already thinking correctly. Isn't that what the devil told you before you became a Christian? Back then you thought you were bright, no one could tell you anything. While you were thinking you were right, you were thinking that it was your thoughts, too.

Little did you know that all the while those thoughts belonged to the devil. All along the thoughts come from the world's system in which you were born. The thoughts come from the philosophy of the devil. They were not your thoughts and they were not godly thoughts either. The thoughts come from the devil.

The devil has a philosophy that he has propagated in this world's system, a way of thinking. From the moment we were born, he tries to sell us that thinking. Some of it we don't even have to learn, some of it just comes out.

When we are born again, the secret of now operating in this new life, this whole new lifestyle, this whole new kingdom that you've gotten into the secret of it, is being able to realize where those old thoughts came from. In truth they were never your thoughts, they belonged to the devil to begin with. He made you think you were thinking those thoughts and doing your own thing. It's not true.

Our thoughts are either influenced by the truth found in God's Word or they're based on the world in which we live. Operating in God's Word is a spiritual experience. It's cooperating with God Who acts on His truth. The Holy Spirit's job is to lead us into all truth.

One of the most intelligent decisions someone can ever make in their life is to accept Jesus as Lord. Why don't we make it sooner? Because we're caught up in this world's system of philosophy. If we were able to think truth all the time, we would have accepted the Lord a long time ago. If you think truth, you'll think like this: God created me. God created this earth. God knows how to make the earth operate. God knows how to make me operate. If I get hooked up with God, I'll operate right.

If we were thinking right, if we were really thinking intelligently all along, that would have been our thought process. But because we have been so influenced by the philosophy that the devil has propagated over the years, it takes us awhile to come around to God's way of thinking.

We have been so influenced by the world's philosophy that the only way we can think intelligently is through the Holy Spirit. The Holy Spirit now has to be the One to intervene and speak truth to us, to cause us to finally see truth. We can't just walk up and accept the Lord without the Holy Spirit. It's the Holy Spirit Who draws us in the first place. Bright as you thought you were, you were not that smart! It was the Holy Spirit Who intervened and got you for that moment in time to think correctly and intelligently enough to make a decision like that.

People cannot make that decision unless they receive divine intervention. If you're praying for someone to be saved, here is one effective way to pray for them: "Lord, please let Your Holy Spirit intervene. Help them to see truth."

Here is the thinking of the world: There is no God so do whatever you want. The Bible says that anyone who says there's no God is a fool. The Bible also tells us something else on this subject: don't be in the presence of such people; some of their foolishness might rub off on you.

Philosophy Number Two: man is a god himself. We don't need God because we're already a god. This is called humanism. If man is God then why is the world in such a mess? Instead of blaming God for the mess of the world, let's put the blame where it belongs: man. People who believe in humanism are generally intellectuals and deep thinkers.

Philosophy Number Three: knowledge is a god. Some people worship knowledge. Think about the philosophers of old who would spend their days talking and thinking and talking some more. They were considered great thinkers. All their thinking was based on their limited knowledge as men. Now how in the world can a created being gain knowledge about his Creator and the creation apart from the Creator? There's no way, it's impossible.

Philosophy Number Four: man can devise his own way to get to God. A lot of people get into trouble with this one. They believe you can do whatever you want to do, whatever road you want to take and still get to heaven. You know, we all just happen to believe a little different, but we'll all get there. You can devise your own way to get there, whatever way suits your nature and your character, whatever way suits your personality. Have you ever heard that garbage? That's a philosophy of the world, it's been propagated by the god of this world and it's a lie.

Philosophy Number Five: all things are relative; there are no absolutes.

As long as we are living in this world, these philosophies will always be here. You will always—even as a Christian—have to make a choice on whether or not to be fooled by one of these philosophies.

One of the reasons this is a problem is that many Christians today don't have the right kind of resolve. We need the kind of resolve that the three Hebrew boys had. Their resolve was this, "We are trusting God." They didn't care what came; they had decided to trust God completely.

Sometimes I get disturbed at what I see happening in today's church. I see people joining the body of Christ simply because they want to be a "good time Christian." A good time Christian is someone who's seeking pleasure after pleasure, thinks only of themselves, and they only want what God can do for them.

They're not concerned about kingdom business, they just want a good time. They want to be with God only when everything is running smooth. When things get a little rough, they're ready to throw in the towel.

The right resolve is when we say, "Lord, I'm going to follow You. I'm going to serve You. I know You're able to do everything You promised, but even if You don't, I'm going to follow You."

There's another kind of Christian–the one with a persecution complex. They see persecution behind every nook and cranny. "Someone's after me. Someone doesn't like me. The devil's on my back."

They're trying to impress God, but what they're really doing is totally out of line with the Word. With their multitude of imagined persecutions they're trying to say, "I've earned the right to be saved, look how I've been persecuted."

Remember, the secret of the kingdom is in the Word of God and the manifestation of His Word in your life. We need to understand that as Christians, we are citizens of another kingdom and we've taken on a new life with new principles. The old principles won't work; the old philosophy of the world will not work in this kingdom. It doesn't transfer because God has other principles. You won't see the power of God in your life unless you operate by His principles that are in His Word.

The knowledge of the secrets of the kingdom of God is that we receive His Word and be fruitful Christians. The very fact that we're born again means that the death of Jesus Christ is a reality to us. It follows then that since His death is a reality to each of us, His new life for us should also be a reality. If His new life is a reality, then the secret of the kingdom—the Word of God—needs to be a reality in our life. It's not a reality until it has changed us.

It's not a reality until it touches us to the point that we're changed men and women of God. That's why when Jesus taught, He wasn't teaching simply to pass the time. He taught so that people would change. When He passed by and saw Zacchaeus, He said, "Come down, I want the truth to change you Zacchaeus."

To us, many times the process of our purpose may seem fruitless, but if we will continue to trust God and remain faithful we will experience His blessings.

PROCESS POINTS

- Process is the designer's suit for purpose.

- Process is the pathway to purpose.

- Process is the plant of God for purpose.

- Process prepares you for purpose.

- Process is the bridge from potential to purpose.

- Process provides for purpose.

- Process is a result of purpose.

Chapter 8
PURPOSE AND PROCESS

"To have faith where you cannot see; to be willing to work on in the dark; to be conscious of the fact that, so long as you strive for the best, there are better things on the way, this in itself is success."

--Katherine Logan

"WHEN GOD'S PURPOSE AND PROCESS MEET, THE END RESULT IS THE FULFILLMENT OF THE WILL OF GOD"

Some years ago when we were building our home, we had several meetings with an architect. At the time I didn't fully appreciate why all the consultations were necessary. However, after the general contractor began the actual building of our home, I came to understand that the architect's drawings were a road map that would bring out a successful end result.

God is like an architect. He always has a plan and always has a purpose for everything He does. In fact, He never does anything without a plan or purpose. When God's purpose and His process come together, we end up with the will of God being accomplished.

God not only views life in terms of the end, but He also speaks in terms of the end even though we're at the beginning. He speaks in terms of the end because He knows He has the ability to take us from the beginning to the end. We need faith because we don't see many times how we're going to get from the beginning to the end. So God gives us faith and faith then becomes the bridge from the beginning of the process to the end.

God's process is always purpose-ful (I want to separate the two words). God's "purpose" is always "full." God began the whole thing in the book of Genesis: *"God blessed them and said to them, be fruitful and increase in number, fill the earth and subdue it; rule over the fish of the sea, the birds of the air"* (Gen. 1:28).

I want you to notice something about God's purpose from the very beginning as we look at the life of Joseph. We will see that God's purpose and His process are designed to bring us to the point where we fulfill His plan. He said to Adam and Eve, "Multiply and fill the earth, and subdue it." In other words, "I want you to make replicas of yourself."

At the time He was saying this to Adam and Eve, they were still in perfect union with Him. So the implication was that when they duplicated themselves, they would in essence be duplicating God. They would be filling the earth with little gods.

From the very beginning God had a purpose for Adam and Eve and for mankind that was greater than themselves. God's purpose is always greater than just you. Simply put: you were not born just for you.

In Genesis 37:1, God is speaking in terms of the end.

> *"Jacob lived in the land where his father had stayed, the land of Canaan. This is the account of Jacob. Joseph, a young man of seventeen, was tending the flocks with his brothers, the sons of Bilhah and the sons of Zilpah, his father's wives; and he brought their father a bad report about them. Now Israel loved Joseph more than any of his other sons, because he had been born to him in his old age."*

I believe that even the birth of Joseph to Jacob in his old age was not by chance. Jacob thought he was finished producing children, but God was just beginning.

"And he (Jacob) made a richly ornamented robe for him (Joseph). When his brothers saw that their father loved him more than any of them, they hated him and could not speak a kind word to him."

The brothers hated Joseph, but do you understand that Joseph had nothing to do with his birth order? It all had to do with the purpose of God. When God has a purpose for someone, it doesn't do any good for us to get all ruffled. We have to appreciate something about God's purpose. God's purpose, as I stated earlier, is not always just for you—it's really for others. Although these brothers were angry at Joseph, because he was born at a certain time, Joseph had nothing to do with it. He was just born, he didn't have a thing to do with it. God had a purpose in mind that was going to bless them.

And then, the Bible says, "Joseph had a dream."

God isn't even paying attention to these brothers. God is moving on with His purpose! If God has given you a glimpse of your purpose, move on with it. Don't waste time listening to the "brothers."

"When he (Joseph) told it to his brothers, they hated him all the more." I don't know if I would have told the brothers the dream. I might have kept that to myself. But Joseph needed to tell it as part of the process.

"He said to them, 'Listen to this dream I had: We were binding sheaves of grain out in the field when suddenly my sheaf rose and stood upright, while your sheaves gathered around mine and bowed down to it.' His brothers said to him, 'Do you intend to reign over us?'"

These brothers understood that Joseph was implying servitude. But what God was doing, though, was revealing the end. They weren't even at the beginning at this point, but God was showing the end.

Verse 9 says, "Then he had another dream, and he told it to his brothers. 'Listen,' he said, 'I had another dream, and this time the sun and moon and eleven stars were bowing down to me.' When he told his father as well as his brothers, his father rebuked him."

God was planting into Joseph's life a vision of the end. I really appreciate the life of Joseph. Never once, having had a glimpse of the end, did he take off prematurely. In God's purpose there is a plan, there's a process, and timing. We don't need to rush it; we don't need to push it–God will bring it to pass.

Joseph was an interesting character. He had those two dreams and shared them with his family, but never once did he try to assert himself over his brothers and say, "Now listen, you remember that dream I had? Well, serve me."

In the purpose of God, there's no need to rush the process because God already has the timing all figured out. Remember, Joseph did not make up these dreams. God gave him the dreams because God wanted him to see the end. Well, if God wanted him to see the end, God knew exactly how He was going to get him to the end. Joseph could relax. He didn't have to be uptight, he didn't have to assert himself or get pushy–he was confident that the God who showed him the end could get him there.

If God has shown you a glimpse of your purpose, just relax. You don't have to remind everybody or attempt to rush things along.

God gets to the beginning of the process in Verse 23: "So when Joseph came to his brothers, they stripped him of his robe—the richly ornamented robe he was wearing—and they took him and threw him into the cistern. Now the cistern was empty; there was no water in it. As they sat down to eat their meal, they looked up and saw a caravan of Ishmaelites coming from Gilead. Their camels were loaded with spices, balm and myrrh, and they were on their way to take them down to Egypt. Judah said to his brothers, *'What will we gain if we kill our brother and cover up his blood?'*"

God's plan was never that Joseph be killed. Little did the brothers know they were cooperating—in their own evil way—with the plan of God. The enemy thinks he's setting us up and he's working us over. He doesn't know that he's just being used.

> *"Come, let's sell him to the Ishmaelites and not lay our hands on him; after all, he is our brother, our own flesh and blood. His brothers agreed. So when the Midianite merchants came by, his brothers pulled Joseph up out of the cistern and sold him for twenty shekels of silver to the Ishmaelites, who took him to Egypt."*

Because of the purpose of God, down went Joseph to Egypt. God had begun His process toward the end of those dreams. You would have thought that if this was God's plan in delivering His people through Joseph, He would have Joseph go to Egypt not as a slave, but on a nice chariot from Pharaoh. Instead, God had a different process for Joseph.

Sometimes God gives you a dream, a little glimpse of your purpose and because the process does not work out quite how you would have put it together, you become discouraged. But I believe that Joseph kept those dreams in his heart. There is no way you could simply forget dreams like that.

I believe sometimes God takes us through a particular process just to show Himself off. It wouldn't have been a big deal if Pharaoh had sent a chariot down and said, "Go pick that boy up and bring him here. I'm going to need him in a while." Instead, Joseph goes down there as a slave. God had the power and He had the plan to get Joseph to the end of that process.

Genesis 39:1 tells us,

> *"Now Joseph had been taken down to Egypt. Potiphar, an Egyptian who was one of Pharaoh's officials, the captain of the guard, bought him from the Ishmaelites who had taken him there. The Lord was with Joseph."*

Once God gives you a glimpse of your purpose, don't get frustrated if things seem to take a wrong turn. God will see you through to the end. The One who shows us the end has the ability to take us from the beginning, through the process, to the very end of it. How comforting that the Bible says, "The Lord was with Joseph."

Do you realize the only reason given for Joseph being elevated from ordinary servant to slave to chief in the house was that "The Lord was with him"? Think about that. There was no other reason given, no other explanation. It indicates to us that the only way we will get to the end of our purpose, is through the ability and power of God. There is no use sitting down and trying to come up with your own plan.

Remember, if you come up with your own strategy, you will have to strategize the rest of your days to stay there. But when it comes to the purpose of God, you can't strategize. God has too unique a plan.

If the Lord is with you, you have enough reason. You don't need anything else, no schemes, no need to manipulate circumstances. If God is with you, He will bring you to the end of your purpose.

"And he lived in the house of his Egyptian master. When his master saw that the Lord was with him and that the Lord gave him success in everything he did."

Look at the only reason Joseph's master, Potiphar, considered him: because God was with him. It wasn't because of his looks; it wasn't because of his intelligence, none of that stuff. Potiphar saw God in Joseph.

"Joseph found favor in his eyes and became his attendant." From a slave to an attendant, all because God was with him. Potiphar put him in charge of his household, look at the training he's going to get now. See, there's a plan in this process, he's being trained and groomed.

"Potiphar put him in charge of his household, and he entrusted to his care everything he owned. From the time he put him in charge of his household and of all that he owned, the Lord blessed the household

of the Egyptian because of Joseph." It didn't say because of Potiphar, it was because of Joseph.

God had shown Joseph the end when he saw the sheaves bow down. He was destined for success. However, it didn't look like that at the beginning of the process, and that's where some of you are right now. It may not look like it; it might look like you're headed for a failure. It may not look like there is a possibility of a blessing, but there is always a blessing in the process of God.

Don't be discouraged by the beginning of the process. That's why God speaks to us about the end, because He wants us to see the end and not focus on the beginning and the middle. You get in the middle and you might not be able to see too much blessing in it. That's why God tells you about the end.

God knew that Joseph was going to be sold into slavery, that's why He showed him the end. God was telling Joseph, "Now just relax, at the end of this process they'll be bowing down to you." When his brothers sold him into slavery Joseph could have said, "Wait, hold on! You said they would bow down to me, not throw me in a hole."

God shows us the end because He knows that when we're in the middle there will be opportunity for discouragement and doubt. Notice that God didn't take away the experience of being sold into slavery. He allowed Joseph to pass through it and experience it.

Joseph moves from a slave to a boss. The only thing he wasn't boss of was Potiphar's wife, and rightly so. But evidently she thought it should be so.

After Joseph had been in prison for a while, he gets released after interpreting dreams for the king. There is something Joseph understood about the purpose of God. He never pushed himself. Now he's in a situation where he's just interpreted the dream for Pharaoh that all of the wise men couldn't interpret. Some people, in Joseph's situation, may have told Pharaoh, "You will notice that I interpreted the dream, so you know that I am the man with the plan." But I want you to see how Joseph was so confident of God's ability to bring him to the end of his purpose, that even in this position, he would not promote himself.

Joseph tells the Pharaoh this in Genesis 41:33:

> "*'And now let Pharaoh look for a discerning and wise man and put him in charge of the land of Egypt. Let Pharaoh appoint commissioners over the land to take a fifth of the harvest of Egypt during the seven years of abundance. They should collect all the food of these good years that are coming and store up the grain under the authority of Pharaoh, to be kept in the cities for food.*

> *"This food should be held in reserve for the country, to be used during the seven years of famine that will come upon Egypt, so that the country may not be ruined by the famine.' The plan seemed good to Pharaoh and to all his officials. So Pharaoh asked them, 'Can we find anyone like this man, one in whom is the Spirit of God?'"*

Pharaoh was no fool. He had sense enough to know that this man Joseph had the Spirit of God on him. You can relax in your purpose. God will bring you to the point where it is fulfilled. People will see that the Lord is with you.

> *"Then Pharaoh said to Joseph, 'Since God has made all this known to you, there is no one so discerning and wise as you. You shall be in charge of my palace, and all my people are to submit to your orders. Only with respect to the throne will I be greater than you."*

First, Potiphar places Joseph in charge of his house and everything except his wife. Now Pharaoh tells Joseph, "The only area I'm going to be greater than you is the throne. Other than that, you are the man. I put you in charge."

> *Verse 42 says, "Then Pharaoh took his signet ring from his finger and put it on Joseph's finger. He dressed him in robes of fine linen and put a gold chain around his neck. He had him ride in a chariot as his second-in-command, and men shouted before him, 'Make way!' Thus he put him in charge of the whole land of Egypt. Then Pharaoh said to Joseph, 'I am Pharaoh, but without your word no one will lift hand or foot in all Egypt'...And Joseph went throughout the land of Egypt.*

"Joseph was thirty years old when he entered the service of Pharaoh king of Egypt. And Joseph went out from Pharaoh's presence and traveled throughout Egypt."

Dropping down to Genesis 47:27 it says,

"Now the Israelites settled in Egypt in the region of Goshen. They acquired property there and were fruitful and increased greatly in number."

Now here is what I want you to understand. In the plan of God, God never has a purpose for your life alone. God's purpose for your life is always tied to the purpose of others. Joseph's purpose was not for Joseph alone.

You were not born just for yourself, you were born for nations. Your purpose was not just for you. God's plan is always that we will touch others with our life. Whatever gifts, whatever talents, whatever abilities God gives you, it's not for you, it's for nations. Although you may not personally touch the nations, the input and contribution from your life could be the seed to assist in the growth of another Joseph.

I often think of the support staff in our ministry. When those men and women operate the cameras, work in the audio tape department, work in the children's church and nursery department, I hope they understand that their purpose is for the nations,

Nations should be touched because you were here. That's why Jacob had a son named Joseph in his old age, not just to increase his family, he had enough. But this one ended up bringing salvation to God's people. When Joseph told them the dream at first they were angry, they said, "What is this fellow trying to say, he's better than we are?" Little did they know that this young man was about to save their lives.

Whenever God uses someone, don't envy them because their life is not for them. Their life could be to open the door for your life, for you to fulfill your purpose. Support them, encourage them.

The brothers thought Joseph was just trying to be smart, "What do you mean, our sheaves bow down to yours?" Even his father didn't understand, saying, "I'm going to serve you?" But when it was all said and done, they bowed to Joseph and gladly so. God had a purpose for Joseph–to save a whole nation.

Whatever God has told you, or will tell you, about your purpose, it is not for you alone. The purpose of Adam and Eve was never for them. That's why God told them to fill the earth because He wanted His righteousness established on the earth.

In 1 Samuel 17—as we discussed earlier in the book—young David battles Goliath. Now, the only reason David went out to fight the Philistine was because the Philistine had defied God. David did not go out there to show off. The only motivation that got him out there was this–Goliath had defied the armies of the living God.

Having been anointed king by Samuel was not what made David go out to battle Goliath. It's not like David was saying, "Let me go out and fight this fellow. I was anointed king, I can handle this."

Way back in 1 Samuel, David had received a vision from God of the end of his purpose. All along he was confident God could bring His purpose to an end, even as God had shown him. So David went through the whole process. At one point he even went into the king's palace and played for him. That would have been a perfect opportunity, some might say, to announce to the king, "By the way, I'm next in line to the throne." But David didn't.

God, in the middle of all of that, was taking David through the process and preparing him for the end. God anointed David king, not for David, but for a nation.

Wherever you are at with God today, I want you to know that God has created you, not for yourself, but for nations. We need to start understanding and seeing our destiny in that manner. Perhaps if we start to see ourselves like that, we will accomplish what the Lord wants us to accomplish.

Our difficulty in the past has been that we don't understand that we were created for others. All our concern has been focused on just ourselves. When we begin to understand that our very purpose has to do with others, it has to do with nations; we begin to reach out to others. We begin to understand the process that we're going through and realize that God is preparing us for His purpose.

At the end of the purpose, He has a goal in mind and He's going to get us there. We don't have to push it, we don't have to rush it, we don't have to impress anyone. We'll get there. They will see in us, they will hear in our speech that the Lord is with us. That was a distinct quality about Joseph and David. You could tell the Lord was with them. Do not allow yourself to become distracted by the accolades of people. When David slew Goliath, brought his head back, the people were rightfully happy, but they went overboard, they lost all sense of respect.

The Bible says, "*The ladies shouted, 'Saul has slain his thousands but David his ten thousands.'*" That just was not a good report.

There was an opportunity there for David to get sidetracked and to jump ahead of God and say, "God, You hear what they're saying. I'm the man! You really did anoint me, now let me go let Saul know what it is."

Even though the people meant well, if David had not been careful, he could have diverted himself from the process of God. He could've tried to get to the purpose of God before the right time.

If you arrive at the end of the purpose before God's time, you arrive without the qualifications. There is nothing like having someone in charge whose not prepared to be in charge. You've seen people in job situations who have some potential, but they're not ready yet for that position. But because of relationship or favoritism they end up in the position. They can't handle it because they're not ready.

That's why Moses had to go tend sheep for awhile. He was just not ready. He had the desire to see his people free, and that was from God. But Moses wanted to end up at the end of his purpose before time. What in the world would he have done if he had succeeded in leading the uprising before the appointed time? Where would he have taken the people? How would he have led them? That would have been a picture of a man who did not go through the process, but wanted to get to the end of the purpose, and it would have been a disaster.

So God blessed him and sent him out there to mind some sheep. If you could put up with the bleating of sheep, you would be able to survive the bleating of those other sheep.

When God gives you a glimpse of the end, relax. He's going to get you to the end of your purpose through the process. He's not going to take the process away, He's going to take you to the end, right through it, and you're going to pass through it, and you're going to get to the end. Because when you get to the end, you have to have the qualifications.

I want to close this book with a special prayer for you. My hope is that it will play a part in helping you to fulfill your destiny in God:

> *"Father in the name of Jesus Christ, I pray for the reader and ask that you will open their eyes to see that what they may be experiencing at this time is only temporary and is simply a step in the process of God.*
>
> *I pray that they will trust your Word to bring them through this process to fulfillment of purpose. I thank you that even what the the adversary meant for evil you will turn around for their good . In Jesus Name,*
>
> *Amen."*